Choose Hope

BY BROOKE TAYLOR

Joined by
An ecumenical community of Christian writers

Project Director:	Brooke Taylor
Managing Editor:	Dr. Trish Berg
Project Coordinators:	Brooke Taylor
	Dr. Trish Berg
	Marie Monsour
	Christina Nieto
Cover Artist:	Adalee Hude
Layout Designer:	Jessica Oswald

Printed and bound in the United States of America.

This book was printed by Total Printing Systems, Inc.,
201 South Gregory Street, Newton, IL, 62448, by Fax 618-783-8407,
by email at sales@tps1.com, and on the internet at www.tps1.com

ISBN-13: 978-0-692-19277-1
ISBN-10: 9 780692 192771

For bulk orders or reorders, please contact
www.brooketaylor.us

Books can also be purchased on www.amazon.com
and from your local bookstore.

Dedication

To anyone in need of hope.

table of Contents

⚓

"Hold fast to the hope that lies before us. This we have as an anchor of the soul, sure and firm, which reaches the interior behind the veil."

-HEBREWS 6:19

Introduction

Human life is a journey. Towards what destination? How do we find the way? Life is like a voyage on the sea of history, often dark and stormy, a voyage in which we watch for the stars that indicate the route. The true stars of our life are the people who have lived good lives. They are lights of hope. Certainly, Jesus Christ is the true light, the sun that has risen above all the shadows of history. But to reach him we also need lights close by—people who shine with his light and so guide us along our way. -Spe Salvi, Pope Emeritus Benedict XVI

I wanted to open the pages of this book with, as you may have expected, a word of hope. The preceding quote is from an encyclical letter entitled "Spe Salvi," which is Latin for "saved in hope," a reference to Romans 8:24: *in hope we are saved.*

Millions of people live in constant anxiety, isolation, pain, and worry about the future. It is important to acknowledge that hope can be difficult. Hope does not presuppose that salvation is easy; in fact, just the opposite. Embracing hope is a recognition of our weakness. In our human frailty and exhaustion, we press on towards something greater. We wait in joyful hope for the coming of our Savior, Jesus Christ.

For a believer of the Way, the storms of life are part of the journey. And sometimes the storms are fierce and unrelenting. That is why the anchor is such a powerful symbol. When the seas rage, it is the anchor that stabilizes the ship. Without it, the vessel could be easily blown off course or overtaken by the waves and capsize. When life feels out of control, it is human nature to try to take hold of something that will keep us upright when the winds are buffeting, pounding us in all directions.

In times of tribulation, what do you grasp?

We pray it is the anchor of hope found only in Jesus.

You can trust that as you drop your anchor below the surface down to the depths, the Rock of Ages will not let you go. At times in our life though, particularly during extreme trials, the nearness of the Lord can be difficult to sense. We need stories of hope, living reminders that there is nothing, *no thing* we have suffered that God's power cannot overcome.

Throughout this book, you will read story after story of how the "stars" in the night sky, real life people, are witnesses to hope through unimaginable loss and adversity. These testimonies are important. During the dark night we can sometimes forget what it looks like to see the sun, even when we know it will rise again. Grief and trials have a way of distorting truth and impairing gratitude. Certain circumstances can isolate us and blind our vision of God's beauty.

I believe the people you will encounter along this 52-week journey will help you persevere, choose hope, and see the glory of what awaits "behind the veil." The Lord sends paracletes and prophets dressed in the skin of ordinary people. It has always been this way. How many souls sailing through a sea of sorrow have been guided by the groans of Job? How many hearts have proclaimed psalms in the pasture with David and wept with Jeremiah? How many have suffered with Jesus?

In our own day and time, the Lord continues to remind us that we are a part of this heritage. An ancestry of hope and resurrection. Within these pages, you will encounter a human constellation, a form of grounded celestial light that reaches to the cosmos and points the way Home.

As I focus on the words of Jesus Christ in John 17:21, I think of His own message of hope: "That they may all be *one*, as you, Father, are in me and I in you, that they also may be in us, that the world may believe that you sent me." This book reminds us to see the living faith dwelling in our brothers and sisters in Christ. That in hope, *we may all be one.*

Choose Hope is an anthology of reflections written by authors from diverse denominational backgrounds. As you read the reflections, you may notice some unfamiliar devotions or prayers. They may seem foreign, but there is great beauty in how Jesus speaks to the believer apart from our own understanding and rituals with which we may be comfortable. We offer these individual stories as an invitation to explore how the Spirit moves beyond borders and walls.

There are many different species of trees in the forest, yet these deciduous disciples praise in unison! They are all rooted in the same life-giving soil. By nature of how they were created, they grow toward heaven and create a dazzling cathedral of praise. We, too, come together in a sea of souls embracing the promises of Christ and the Resurrection with our own unique journey. Through these graces shared by our writers, an outpouring of hope is born.

***

I would like to offer heartfelt thanks to our writers. In some cases, in order to bring you their stories, some have recounted the worst day of their lives. Hope was found in the depths of that pain, but it is a costly request to ask of them. The writing process can be emotionally draining. From my heart, I thank our contributors for rising to this challenge and giving their "Yes" to be a part of *Choose Hope*.

Special thanks to Adalee from Brightly Hude Studio for the beautiful cover art, Lisa Walters for proofreading, and Jessica Oswald for the page layout. Most especially, I am indebted to the managing editor of this project, Trish Berg, and our *Choose Hope* team including Marie Monsour and Christina Nieto, for their patience, diligence, and dedication.

The Lord Our Justice

-MIGUEL CHAVEZ

The days are coming—oracle of the Lord—when I will fulfill the promise I made to the house of Israel and the house of Judah. In those days, at that time, I will make a just shoot spring up for David; he shall do what is right and just in the land. In those days Judah shall be saved and Jerusalem shall dwell safely; this is the name they shall call her: "The Lord our justice."

JEREMIAH 33:14-16

Justice is certainly a prevalent theme throughout Sacred Scripture and is often used to describe *how* God acts.

As we begin the season of Advent, we prepare our hearts to welcome Christ who is *Emmanuel*, God with us. Through the incarnation, God becomes flesh and brings redemption and salvation to the world. His grace and love pour into our lives, transforming what is ordinary and limited to the extra-ordinary and sublime. In a culture of death, He brings life. He is light in darkness and hope in times of hopelessness.

The Lord is justice! Justice involves *seeing* the world how *God sees* the world, recognizing the glimmers of truth and beauty that shine through the darkness and brokenness we encounter. I am reminded of a story of *brokenness*.

One hot afternoon, my young son, desiring some water, reached into the cupboard and pulled a tall glass down. His little fingers seemed like butter as he desperately clenched the glass, and it slipped right to the floor, shattering into pieces. I immediately told him to freeze as I gathered the broom and diligently swept up the broken shards of glass that covered the floor. As I gazed at what seemed like hundreds of little pieces of glass in my dustpan, I marveled at how quickly a useful item in the house could become broken, useless and even dangerous.

As I threw the shards of glass into the trash, I remembered a memory of when I was younger, playing with an older kaleidoscope. When you hold a kaleidoscope in the light, its contents come together and give the optic of a beautiful and intricate design. As you rotate the kaleidoscope, the designs through the eyepiece change and seem even more beautiful.

Curious, I tried to discover what was inside and broke open the cylinder. To my surprise, its contents were simply mirrors and broken shards of colorful glass. When glass breaks, we often deem it as dangerous and worthless, and we are quick to sweep it up and throw it away. In an older kaleidoscope, the opposite seems true. It *requires* the broken glass and mirrors to create the beautiful designs. It uses what was broken and "worthless" to create meaningful and beautiful patterns for the beholder.

Seeing the world as God sees it can be incredibly challenging at times. It often requires that our perception sink below what is simply on the surface. We are God's beloved, made in His image and likeness and called to share His love with all we meet. We are called to use our gifts and talents for the betterment of others, especially those who suffer and have little.

Unfortunately, sin often clouds our vision and illusion takes the place of reality. We must not be fooled by what the world offers us. Sin is the root of our disconnectedness with God and the source of our brokenness and insecurity.

It's easy to encounter brokenness in the world. When you encounter the poor and displaced, the sick and the helpless, the lonely and grieving, the outcast and lost, these are encounters of brokenness. Perhaps we wrestle with our own deficiencies and insecurities as brokenness in our own lives. Brokenness often leaves us feeling worthless and meaningless, like the shattered glass.

God's justice, how God *sees the world*, is more like the kaleidoscope. He takes the brokenness in our lives and, like shards of colorful glass in a kaleidoscope, He arranges them intentionally, with purpose, so that when held in the light of faith, these broken pieces reveal the most beautiful designs. *This* is God's justice!

Reflecting on the reading:

1. Have you encountered brokenness this week? Injustice?

2. How did you react?

3. How can you see the broken as God sees them, more like the kaleidoscope of beauty and purpose?

Weekly readings: Jeremiah 33:14–16; Psalm 25:4–5, 8–9, 10, 14;
1 Thessalonians 3:12–4:2; Luke 21:25–28, 34–36

May His Love Overflow
-KELLY LILAK

And this is my prayer: that your love may increase ever more
and more in knowledge and every kind of perception.

PHILIPPIANS 1:9

"Excuse me, do you know where the nearest water fountain is?" A stranger pointed across the field at a distant drinking fountain. "Oh, no, I meant a *BIG* fountain!" He then guided me in a different direction.

As I was praying with the mass readings for the second week of Advent, the verse that describes God's love overflowing, or increasing, kept coming up throughout the following weeks of prayer. This image touched my soul: that God pours His love into us, and by the power of the Holy Spirit that love overflows, touching others and flowing back to Him.

It's like that fountain I saw at the park. I sat there contemplating how it worked and as I did, the wind blew and water splashed on me, on the grass, on the hard stone, and some splashed back into the water flow. God yearns to pour His love into our lives and He yearns for us to simply receive it. He wants to give us Himself - His life, love, joy, peace, strength and hope. He invites us to a continual love relationship with Him, but this love relationship is not meant to be just between God and us. We are called to share His love with all those around us.

This is why Jesus was born into this world - because of His profound, unlimited, never-ending love for us. As I walked and prayed around that fountain, I thought about how common it is for people to throw in coins and make a wish. I decided to toss in my own coins, not for a wish, but a prayerful hope.

As I reached into my purse to find three pennies (one for the Father, the Son and the Holy Spirit), I realized that what I hoped for has already been given to me: Jesus Christ Himself and His never-ending love and mercy. Suddenly, as I felt those three pennies in my hand, I felt tremendous gratitude fill my soul.

God invites us to be in union and communion with Him every day. He invites us to the heavenly banquet of the holy sacrifice of the Mass, which happens throughout the world, every hour of the day. He invites us through prayer, scripture, communion with each other and the sacraments.

I hope to be in continual union with Him. I hope that I can imitate our Blessed Mother by being God's vessel of love, receiving Christ in me so that His love overflows in me, and through me reaches others in my life. I hope others will know how much they are loved by Him.

My prayer for you as we continue to prepare the way for the Lord this advent season is that you receive Christ and His love for you. That you feel His love overflow in your soul and that you always seek His ways. He is our hope, our source, our Savior, our healer, our fountain, our life, our all in all. He can quench your thirst. He forgives all your sins, loves you profoundly, and gives you Himself. May His love overflow in you more and more each day.

Reflecting on the reading:

1. Has there been a time in your life when you felt God's love overflow in your soul?

2. Have you ever been blessed by someone else and felt God's love through them?

3. How can you pray this week to receive God's love and allow it to overflow and touch those around you?

Weekly readings: Baruch 5:1-9; Psalm 126:1-6; Philippians 1:4-6, 8-11; Luke 3:1-6

A Million Little Blessings
-CAITIE BEARDMORE

Rejoice in the Lord always. I shall say it again: rejoice!
PHILIPPIANS 4:4

A few years ago, I had the opportunity to go on an all-expenses-paid trip to Italy. Everything from my plane ticket to my hotel was covered and I was going with a group of people I adore! I should have been over the moon, but I was paralyzed with anxiety.

I was nervous that I would feel claustrophobic with forty people on a bus, as I typically depend on my quiet time. I had heard that the group typically walked over ten miles a day, mostly uphill, and I have terrible knee trouble. I was told the weather would be over ninety degrees, and I prefer cooler weather. I did not have the right clothes. I easily get motion sickness. And the list goes on.

As our departure date loomed, the knots in my stomach grew tighter. I began to pray my favorite one-line prayer over and over: "Steady me, Jesus. Steady me, Jesus. Steady me, Jesus." When it came time to go, I felt God's presence on the flight as He sat me next to one of my favorite kids. She distracted me from my worries and kept my mind on things above. The bus ride brought new anxieties, and though I did get motion sickness, I also felt God's presence. My prayer became a prayer of thanksgiving: "Thank You, Jesus!"

On each day of this journey, I saw a million little blessings from above. And though each new situation made me anxious, I prayed, and I felt Jesus deliver me graciously. With God's grace, even awkward moments became pretty funny!

One that I will never forget happened while we were standing outside of Cardinal Dolan's favorite restaurant in Rome. Suddenly, a pigeon pooped right on my head and I screamed out a bad word. I was absolutely mortified and I ran into the restaurant while everyone else laughed hysterically. Eventually, I was able to see the humor in that catastrophe, and now we even speak to each other in pigeon memes.

During this trip, I wasted two weeks in one of the most beautiful countries in the world being hesitant and anxious when God was able to take "bad moments" and make them beautiful. This realization changed my life forever. I realized that God would always deliver me from my fears. After all, He delivered Sarah from infertility and made Abraham the father of nations! He delivered the Israelites from Pharaoh's reign in Egypt and made them the chosen people! He sent His Son to die for us and delivered us from sin to inherit His kingdom! How could I have ever doubted this?

The biggest lesson I brought home from Rome was that choosing hope and joy takes practice. Like a doctor practices medicine and a Christian practices their faith, I started to practice choosing hope and joy. Each time I am faced with a situation that makes me feel anxious, I stop, pray and cling to God. I remember how God delivered me from all of my fears in Rome, and I trust in Him to deliver me again. I don't always do this well, but I lean on the one-liner prayers like "Steady me, Jesus" followed by a "Thank You, Jesus."

And though I am still a work in progress, I have allowed my overseas journey to change my thought process in this life. Now, when I am faced with a stressful situation, my first reaction is faith instead of fear. Trust instead of turmoil. And each day I journey through this life, I will choose hope and never again waste another day in His glory.

Reflecting on the reading:

1. *Has there ever been a time in your life when you felt anxious or stressed?*
2. *How did you choose to handle the anxiety? Did that help?*
3. *How can you pray for God to help you trust in Him in those moments of anxiety?*

Weekly readings: Zephaniah 3:14-18a; Isaiah 12:2-6; Philippians 4:4-7; Luke 3:10-18

Trusting in Jesus

-CORINA BARRANCO

Blessed are you who believed that what was spoken to you by the Lord would be fulfilled.

LUKE 1:45

Believing in God, trusting in Jesus, was not an easy decision for me to make. At a young age, I discovered God's love and compassion, but truly trusting in Him came later in my life through seeing how God blessed my family and helped us through many difficulties.

I was only five years old when I crossed the border with my mother to migrate to the United States of America in search of a better life. My mother and I risked our lives leaving our home country and crossing the border with strangers. A day before we left Mexico, my mother and I went to church and we prayed to God, asking Him to protect us as we put our lives in His hands. We had faith that He was going to be with us every step of the way. Although I was still very young and didn't quite comprehend what it meant to have faith, I looked up to my mother and found confidence and peace that could only come from God.

We arrived safe and sound to the United States and started our brand new life. However, adapting to a new lifestyle was very difficult for us. For my parents, it was very hard finding work because they did not have social security numbers. Nonetheless, my parents did not give up. Eventually my father found a job in a restaurant, working under the table as a dishwasher and my mother found a job as a cleaning lady. My parents worked hard to make ends meet, and I admire them for never giving up. At that point, I was too young to understand that their strength and hope came from their faith in Jesus.

Growing up, my parents didn't own a car and it was a struggle to get places. During the winter months, we all suffered because in order to get places we had to walk in the harsh weather conditions. Transportation was not easy to find and we always had a challenge finding someone to take us where we needed to go. My mother hated asking for rides because she always felt like she was a bother. Unfortunately, our church was not walking distance and there was no public transportation. My mother always tried her best to make sure that we had a ride to church; she made that a priority.

As the years went by, I started to become upset and even angry with God because I felt like our struggles were so unfair. Some days, I would throw myself on my bed and just cry and cry, feeling sorry for myself. I was impatient and somehow felt like God had forgotten about my family. My problem was that I was too focused on what I didn't have rather than counting the blessings I did have.

I began to thank God for all the blessings we had, and eventually, I began to trust God for providing for our needs. I began to see that His ways were not always my ways and His time was not always my time. I began to trust God and knew that I had to be patient. I knew that someday I would own my own car. Someday I would have a better life.

I am now eighteen years old and I own my own car. I can now take my mother places and it makes life so much easier for us. This is just one of the many blessings I have received from the Lord, all because I decided to have faith and trust in Him.

Believing in God and trusting in Jesus is what we need in this life. God has so much in store for us because He knows what we need and what is best for us. We are blessed because we believe; no matter what we face in this life, God is there.

Reflecting on the reading:

1. Looking back, how many times have you reproached the Lord for something you don't have?

2. How can you embrace having a thankful heart?

3. This week, how will you reflect your gratitude to God in your prayers?

Weekly readings: Micah 5:1-4a; Psalm 80:2-3, 15-16, 18-19; Hebrews 10:5-10; Luke 1:39-45

Christmas Day
-BROTHER RICHARD HENDRICK

When they saw this, they made known the message
that had been told them about this child.
LUKE 2:17

It was a long winter that year; January seemed unending. It was a winter made longer by the coldness within our home rather than the coldness without. Long gray days stretched in front of us and dark skies seemed to rest only a few inches above our heads. After a number of ever more fractious years, our family was in a freefall of separation leading to the chaos of emotions, recriminations, and at times, the borderlands of despair that such wounds bring.

Christmas had been a disaster. No peace and joy to all in our home that year. Only pain seemed to be on the horizon. God seemed to be missing.

We had been a "good practicing Catholic family," so surely this was not supposed to happen to us, was it?

In the midst of the anger and pain, we were raising fundamental questions of trust in God and in one another which seemed to remain unanswered. Prayer seemed to be only an exercise in frustration, a way of coming upon a steel gray door that was shut firmly between heaven and here, leaving one leaning upon it exhausted or banging upon it in anger.

Then it happened.

One morning after another long night of tears, and anger, and pain, I came down to the kitchen early to make tea. I filled the kettle at the sink, my tired eyes blearily looking out at the muddy gray vista that passed for a garden. A glint of shining gold suddenly caught my eye and woke me up. There, beneath the old cherry tree that never produced any fruit, was a tiny flame wavering in the wind. A crocus flower! It had bloomed overnight where, in all the past winters in that house, there had never been a flower before.

Watching it, seeing it there in the midst of the wintered garden, I felt hope rise in my heart for the first time in weeks. Not hope for anything in particular but simply the *ability* to hope. To choose to hope. It seemed impossible that in that cold gray garden, the earth held the light of the sun, a living promise of a spring that would definitely, eventually, come - not just to the garden out there, but to the garden of hearts in here.

In that moment, no angel had a halo so bright, no votive candle shone so splendidly, as that little crocus did.

And after hope, it brought joy.

Slowly the house woke up to the reality of our little visitor outside. Each morning we checked to see if it was still there, chatted about its purpose, and wondered how it had grown in the midst of the snow. As we chatted, each of us was simply happy that it was there.

We saw in it no promise of particular resolution, rather, a simple reminder that in the state of our pain, in the winter of our hearts, Jesus deeply buries the seeds of spring.

After all, the One who is our first hope chose the darkest midwinter to be born and the deepest spring to rise again, becoming for us the first seed of resurrection for all of creation and inviting those who entered that dark cave of a stable to choose to bring hope to the world again.

Over the next three years, we still went through more trauma, more pain, more questioning. The little miracles, like our crocus, come not to help us avoid suffering, but to help us transcend it and grow through it. For a few years, around Christmastide, our little crocus shined the light of hope into our house and into our hearts. Then one year, once we found balance again, we noticed that the crocus did not bloom.

It seems that little crocus, like angels, are only with us for as long as we need them - to remind us of God's never ending love, and to teach us to choose hope.

Reflecting on the reading:

1. What family struggles have burdened your life this year, making celebrating Christmas difficult?

2. What little miracles are all around you, reminding you of God's love and grace?

3. How can you choose hope this Christmastime and all year through?

Weekly readings: Isaiah 62:11-12; Psalm 97:1, 6, 11-12; Titus 3:4-7; Luke 2:15-20

Life is Like a Puzzle
-JOAN SPIETH

Blessed are all who fear the Lord, and who walk in his ways.
PSALM 128:1

Have you ever wondered why life sometimes feels like a puzzle? As if we are trying to snap pieces into place without seeing the whole picture? It's not only *my* musing, I have spoken to many other friends who have asked the same question to God. As I sat down to write my reflection, I felt lost for words. I sought to find a starting point to write my assigned piece for the book, and the Bible verses that were assigned to me included the feast of the Holy Family of Jesus, Mary, and Joseph. Suddenly, I felt excited to write my reflection as these verses held a special place in my heart. I often run to them with pleas in prayers.

Even with the excitement of my assigned scripture verses, I was still left clueless. Weeks passed, and the submission deadline loomed. My thoughts screamed, *no way, just throw in the towel.* Then a friend said, "Ask for more time." Those four words made me reconsider. Those four words changed my attitude. Those four words offered encouragement, and that is when I became prayerfully open to writing a reflection on the Feast of the Holy Family.

Two strong trains of thought came to the fore: the cross and the expression of joy on St. Joseph's face in two separate and favorite depictions of the Holy Family fleeing to Egypt. Aha! Now the puzzle pieces were fitting. Returning to the list of scriptures, I read first Psalm 128:1, "Blessed are all who fear the Lord, who walk in obedience to Him." I knew that was it!

In the rite of the night, the Holy Family had prayed with holy offerings of praise and thanksgiving. They settled into place, in full repose. Joseph was bolted from that repose by the angel's message. He was to flee with his beloved Mary and the son of the Most High God. To flee, because the danger was great and most imminent. The compelling force that had urged them to set out towards Egypt now lessened; still present, yes, but it was now allowing them to breathe.

The light from the moon aided their spirits and the footing for both Joseph and their donkey. It also, for a few moments, brought into distinct focus a young tree. The shadow it cast was in the form of a cross. When Mary and Joseph saw it, they immediately knew its meaning.

> "The Cross is foolishness to those who perish
> But for us it has become the wisdom of God
> The Cross is foolishness to those who perish
> But for us it is salvation and power from God"
>
> *("The Cross Is Foolishness" Lyrics by John Michael Talbot | album The Troubadour Years)*

When life seems to be like a puzzle of jumbled pieces and mismatched connections, we can find our hope in the foolishness of the cross. The cross signifies our hope that leads to triumph. We are called in our faithfulness to pick up our cross and carry it with the joyful strength of Joseph, the peaceful strength of Mary, and the sure-footed strength of their donkey. And that is when all of the puzzle pieces will fit together.

Reflecting on the reading:

1. Has your life ever felt like a jumbled puzzle?

2. How can you find your hope in the foolishness of the cross?

3. How can your prayers reflect your hope in the cross even in the midst of troubles?

Weekly readings: 1 Samuel 1:20-22, 24-28; Psalm 128:1-5; 1 John 3:1-2, 21-24; Luke 2:41-52

three things

-CHERI KEAGGY

Arise! Shine, for your light has come, the glory of the Lord has dawned upon you.
ISAIAH 60:1

I'll never forget it. My life as I knew it was falling apart. After years of significant struggle, my twenty-two-year marriage to my high school sweetheart was ending. At a time when I could barely speak the word divorce, that's exactly what we were facing.

There I sat one evening in a pit of despair, completely overwhelmed by my circumstances. Racked with pain and riddled with fear, I knew enough to get myself to church. Defeated, waiting for the service to begin, I was drowning in a flood of unanswered questions. Why won't he fight for me? Will I be single the rest of my life or would God miraculously heal our marriage as I had prayed, fasted and believed for so long?

That night, God met me through the faithful preaching of my pastor. He shared a simple message on the three things we need to survive. I was definitely in survival mode, desperate for a nugget of hope to cling to. My pastor shared that what we need to survive is air, sustenance (food/water), and God's presence.

As I counted up his list, I realized I had all three. In that moment, I knew that the God who sees all - saw me - and I had everything I needed in Christ. While I still did not have all the answers, I realized I didn't have to, as long as He did. I understood like never before that God's grace was sufficient for me, and Jesus was enough.

That summer, as the dust was still settling from all that had transpired, I was scheduled to sing at a women's conference. God's marching orders aren't always crystal clear as we seek Him for our next steps. But that weekend, there was no confusion whatsoever. After a long songwriting drought, God had made it clear that upon returning home I was to begin writing again.

The first fruits of obedience was a song called "Air, Food, and Water" which I later recorded on an album full of healing songs called So I Can Tell. I refer to it as my "beauty from ashes" project. Later, as God saw fit, He further redeemed my story by bringing me a new husband. We wrote a new song titled "Restoration Song," and we were able to sing it together at our wedding.

Yes, God is in the business of healing broken hearts.

Is there a place in your heart that is broken? Are you in need of God's healing? While others may fail or abandon you, there is One who will never leave or forsake you. There is One who can bring beauty from the ashes of your life. Dear friend, by God's grace and equipping, no matter what, choose hope.

I did, and it has made all the difference.

SO I CAN TELL

I was shown grace, so I will be gracious

I was shown mercy, so I will be merciful and kind

I have been loved, to be lovely, yes, but that I might love well

I have heard the Truth so I can tell

I have known pain, and though it was painful

I have been healed, now I am speaking healing words

You gave me strength to be strong enough to carry someone else

I have heard the Truth so I can tell

Tell it to my neighbor, tell it to my brother, tell it to the woman down the street

Tell it to the children, tell it to the broken, live it so that everyone can see

My Jesus, the Love that came to dwell inside of me, so that others might believe

I have known joy, so I can be joyful

Been broken down, but now I'm breaking free

You gave me faith to be faithful, yes, no matter how I felt

I have heard the Truth so I can tell

I have heard the Truth

It's the least I can do

I have heard the Truth so I can tell

Written by Cheri Keaggy
Copyright 2012 So I Can Tell Publishing (BMI)

Reflecting on the reading:

1. *When was your heart broken, abandoned by someone in your life?*

2. *How did you allow God to heal your heart?*

3. *How can you seek God's healing for past pain and trust God for His love?*

Weekly readings: Isaiah 60:1-6; Psalm 72:1-2, 7-8, 10-13; Ephesians 3:2-3a, 5-6; Matthew 2:1-12

A Year of Transformation
-YOLANDA MALDONADO

The voice of the Lord is over the waters; the God of glory thunders, the Lord, over the mighty waters. The voice of the Lord is power; the voice of the Lord is splendor.

PSALM 29:3-4

A year ago I became a stay-at-home mom. That simple sentence is a dream come true, a gift from God. After many years of struggling with infertility and then a divorce in my thirties, I was broken and thought I would never be a mom. But God had a plan and it was worth waiting for. He brought a long-lost love back into my life who was eager to marry me and hoped to have babies with me. Not only that, He also brought me back into communion with the Catholic Church and literally renewed both of our lives.

So there I was, ready to be home with my son and daughter and selfishly just enjoy life. But God had a plan and, looking back now, it was another gift. He had given me this time and flexibility to be with my aging parents, in a year that my dad would steadily decline from illness and ultimately be called to Heaven's gates. But let me go back a bit.

The verse "Give to the Lord, you sons of God, give to the Lord glory and might" reminds me of my dad. He was a strong and courageous man of God, a deacon in our church and pillar of our family; he was passionate about giving glory to God. He gave his homilies with a thunderous zeal for our Lord. Nothing deterred my dad's love and appreciation for the Lord. When illness swept over his life, first pancreatic cancer, his faith remained steadfast through surgery and chemotherapy and by the grace of God, he beat cancer. Then slowly dementia crept in and Alzheimer's took over, but the Lord always remained the source of his hope.

Within a couple months of my being home, my dad had an episode that landed him in the hospital, then a nursing home facility for rehabilitation and home again. This wasn't the first time this had happened but we had no idea that this was the beginning of his descent. I was able to be there to help my mom who was my dad's main caregiver, take them to doctor's appointments, grocery shop and help with anything that was needed. Often times with my little ones in tow.

My prayer life was strengthened because I couldn't do this on my own. Most days I was exhausted just from trying to be a good mom to my 3 and 1-year-old. I prayed for perseverance, to be able to gracefully handle what was needed of me so that I could bring comfort to my mom and dad. I was being called to serve my parents. I embraced the commandment, honor your mother and father. And I came to understand the saying by Saint Teresa of Calcutta, "We can do no great things, only small things with great love."

Eventually, we realized hospice was the best thing for him. Then just a few months later, a stroke left him in bed, immobilized and his speech incomprehensible. This heartbreaking state that my father was in allowed me, for the first time, to really see and learn to respect the dignity in the brokenness of the body. It also allowed me to see the love of our Blessed Mother Mary in my mom's actions as she cared for my dad--bathing him, feeding him, comforting him, singing to him, praying with him. Seeing her love and compassion for him made it easier to follow her lead as my siblings and I helped her care for him. All the while, a peace that can only come from God permeated their home.

The details of the way the Lord called my dad home are so beautiful that I have tucked them away in my heart to treasure. He passed so peacefully, as we sang songs of praise to our God, that any fear I ever had of death has been washed away. My dad's devotion and service to our Lord were evident in the sacredness of his death. Although illness stripped him bare, all I see is the glory in God's promises to those that belong to Him.

Reflecting on the reading:

1. *In the storms of life, how do you give glory to God?*

2. *What do you do in times of trouble to stay close to the Lord?*

3. *How can you pray for peace and patience with the life you are living and the God you worship?*

   Weekly readings: Isaiah 40:1-5, 9-11; Psalm 29:1-4, 9-10;
   Titus 2:11-14; 3:4-7; Luke 3:15-16, 21-22

In Between

-DR. TRISH BERG

Jesus did this as the beginning of his signs in Cana in Galilee
and so revealed his glory, and his disciples began to believe in him.
JOHN 2:11

My dad was born on January 15, 1933. He died in 1997. In between, he lived a life without truly knowing love and forgiveness, without knowing Jesus.

I have many memories of my dad; most of them are not sweet ones. But among the dark shadows, there are a few good memories. I remember Dad playing "Skip to My Lou" on his guitar as my older sister and I skipped in circles in our ranch house basement. I remember driving with him from Ohio to New York in his little yellow Honda Civic to visit my grandparents. And I remember him walking me down the aisle at my wedding and giving me a final kiss at the altar.

I also remember never feeling loved by my dad. Whatever I did it was never enough for him to accept me. At the age of nine, I sat with Dad watching *Nadia Comaneci* become the first gymnast in Olympic history to be awarded the perfect score of ten. I remember my dad's complete admiration of her. The next day, desperately trying to please my dad, I asked him to sign me up for gymnastic lessons. He did, but let's just say it did not go well.

My parents fought a lot, and my dad often used my tears to get at my mom by threatening to leave us. I have numerous memories of standing at the front porch screen door crying, watching him toss his suitcase into the trunk of that yellow Honda Civic, begging him not to go.

My parents divorced when I was ten, and my dad moved to Florida. My heart ached again for the love I never received from him that was now even more out of reach.

At twenty, I met the love of my life, Michael, and we married a few years later. Michael introduced me to Jesus Christ. I saw him live for Jesus, and I wanted what he had. Through Jesus, I found hope like I had never known, and love like I could never have imagined.

We often spoke to my dad about Jesus' love and forgiveness, but he loved to argue specific biblical facts. Then, in 1997, he came down with pneumonia, and after a few weeks, we knew he was not likely to recover. His breathing became more labored and his life was slipping away.

My dad knew he was dying, and he knew he needed Jesus. He finally opened his heart to God, and came to faith in Christ just two days before he died. Knowing he was a broken man, one of the last things he said to me was that all he had left was Jesus and his two daughters.

I told him that was all he needed.

On a chilly Wednesday in November, my dad went home, and finally found the peace he never had in his "in between."

Our God is the God of miracles, the God of hope. When Jesus turned water into wine at the wedding in Cana, it was the "first of the signs through which he revealed his glory" (John 2:1-11). At the age of thirty, this was His first miracle. At the age of thirty-three, Jesus was crucified, died, was buried, and on the third day He rose again.

In between, and forevermore, He works miracles, He gives us hope.

I was born in 1968, and have no idea when I will die. In between I have found a way to forgive my dad, and in so doing, have found the hope that can only come from God.

And though my dad did not live with Christ, he did die with Christ, and maybe that's the only in between that really matters.

Reflecting on the reading:

1. *What childhood memories mean the most to you?*

2. *How has your relationship with your earthly father impacted your faith?*

3. *What is the most important aspect of your "in between"?*

Weekly readings: Isaiah 62:1-5; Psalm 96:1-3, 7-10; 1 Corinthians 12:4-11; John 2:1-11

One Body One Hope

-JEN GERBER

As a body is one though it has many parts, and all the parts of the body, though many, are one body, so also Christ. For in one Spirit we were all baptized into one body, whether Jews or Greeks, slaves or free persons, and we were all given to drink of one Spirit.

1 CORINTHIANS 12:12-13

"Mom, do you think that I could ever be a saint?"

Evie's words are forever etched in my mind and I retrieve them when I am weary from living out my vocation as a homeschooling mother. Exhausted by energetic and clingy toddlers and the demands of being both a parent and a teacher, I am sometimes tempted to skip our daily reading about the life of a saint and move on to more pressing matters like math and cleaning the toilet.

But then I think about my sweet daughter and hear her voice asking this question almost weekly as we learned about the heroic men and women who loved Jesus and helped Him build His Church. I thought I had a lifetime to introduce them to her. Little did I know she would only be given eleven short years on this earth.

Some of the men and women we read about moved mountains for Jesus. Joan of Arc helped save her native France from English domination. Saint Benedict founded monasticism and developed a Rule of life. The Apostle Peter built the very foundations of a Church that is still living and breathing to this day.

Even though these saints were beloved to the Church and to our own family, I would often see a look of discouragement creep across her face as we read about their obvious and monumental contributions to Christianity.

"But what about me?" she wondered.

I always tried to encourage her in these moments, to remind her that God calls all of us to sainthood no matter where we live and what we do. A saint is simply someone who faithfully serves Christ by giving their "yes" to God in each moment, even the seemingly mundane ones.

Ironically, it would be the life of another saint that would quell her discouragement - St. Therese of Lisieux.

In Therese, Evie recognized a simple and steadfast faith at the heart of sainthood. Although she was not an apostle, and did not found a religious order or charitable organization, she lived out her faith in a most extraordinary way by performing small acts of kindness with great love. And though Saint Therese died at the age of twenty-four, her "little way" (as she coined it), would be the inspiration for myriads of Christians everywhere.

As Evie matured, I witnessed the seeds of St. Therese's simple message blossoming in her soul. Her siblings' chores would mysteriously be completed without their knowledge. She would concede if there was a disagreement over which game to play or who would get the last cookie. It seemed when a need arose, Evie recognized it and did what she could to help. She hated to see anyone left out and had a tender heart for kids with special needs, the lonely, and the marginalized.

At our homeschooling co-op, she formed a Rosary group that would meet during recess to pray. When one friend forgot her rosary, she made a beaded bracelet for her so that she would always have one close at hand. One of her most endearing qualities was her knack for leaving little love notes all over the house to encourage her family. Even three years after her death, we are still finding her messages and they have become sacred relics of her compassionate heart.

Unfortunately, Evie did not live long enough to fully discern what role she would play as a member of Christ's body. Like her hero, Saint Therese, she learned to serve others with love and humility from where she was. Evie's love for Jesus and others has had a lasting impact on everyone who had the privilege of knowing her.

Whether God calls us to be a great teacher or simply the one who sweeps the floor, we all have an important role to play in building up the body of Christ. No part can be discarded or survive without the support of the others. And together, all of the parts act as a singular witness to hope for a lost and broken world.

Reflecting on the reading:

1. Have you ever felt small, like your efforts were not seen by others?

2. What can you do this week to show Christ's love to others like Evie and Saint Therese?

3. How can your prayer life reflect your thankfulness for others' small sacrifices?

Weekly readings: Nehemiah 8:2–4a, 5-6, 8-10; Psalm 19:8-10, 15;
1 Corinthians 12:12–30; Luke 1:1–4; 4:14-21

Just a Sinner-Saved by Grace

- AUTUMN MANKINS

I chose you before I formed you in the womb; I set you apart
before you were born. I appointed you a prophet to the nations.
JEREMIAH 1:5

The floors creak beneath my feet as I slowly make my way to the kitchen. My coffee brews while the refrigerator softly hums in the background. I push open the window to hear the birds chirping and see the sun just beginning to peak above the tree line. The grass is glistening in the sunlight, still damp from the early morning dew. Both kids are still snoozing in their beds so I grab my Bible and head to my favorite seat in the house. While I wait on my coffee, I open my Bible and find my place from the previous morning. I usually muster a sleepy "Good morning, Lord. Open my heart to what you have for me," and begin to read.

It's in this quiet, serene time of day that God has done the most shattering work on my heart. Since becoming a stay-at-home-mom almost four years ago, I have struggled with my new identity. I have started businesses, picked up hobbies, and renovated 90% of our home. While I still enjoy all of these things, they never quite brought the fulfillment, identity, or prestige that I expected.

I grew up in the church, so I am all too familiar with the concept of finding my identity in Christ alone. I know this is the answer. As a woman, I have a tendency to put pressures on myself that really don't exist. Pressures to impress others or have a career that screams success. In my efforts to become who I think others want me to be, I lose sight of who I know Jesus wants me to be.

I have great news, friends. Jesus doesn't care if we're CEOs in business suits or soccer moms struggling to find matching socks. He doesn't need us to be in charge of 30 organizations all while baking fresh pies, never washing the same load of laundry twice, and having a social media worthy home.

Jesus just wants our heart. He wants us to love spending time with Him and desire to further His kingdom. Jesus wants us to seek His will for our lives without reservation. He calls us to invest in our husbands and children daily. He calls us to come to Him when we're messy and strip away the things in our lives that aren't there to honor Him. And guess what? In this season of my life, none of these things require a fancy title. All I have to be is Autumn – a sinner saved by grace.

I love that. A sinner saved by grace. A friend recently told me that was how her Grandma Ruth always introduced herself. Maybe I should try it. "Hi, I'm Autumn and I'm just a sinner saved by grace."

There is so much beauty and simplicity in that identity. It strips away all of the expectations placed on us. ALL we have to be is a sinner saved by grace. It doesn't require any work, any degrees, any level of skill. All that is required of us is for our hope and our future to be in the Lord.

Jeremiah 1:5 reads: "I chose you before I formed you in the womb; I set you apart before you were born. I appointed you a prophet to the nations."

Jesus chose you. He formed you. He set you apart. The Lord created you for a specific purpose. His plans for you might be eating picnic lunches off of the kitchen floor on a rainy day with your kids. The plans might include delivering a meal to a hurting friend or volunteering weekly at the church. Our life purpose may be to serve others and, in turn, teach our children to serve others. Maybe your place is in an office showing the Lord's love to your coworkers. Maybe your place is in the schools, teaching the next generation. Or maybe, like me, your place is in the home. Wherever you are, just be in God's will. It's the safest place to be.

So, I'd like to introduce myself. My name is Autumn. I am a mom. I am a wife. I am a friend. But most of all…I'm just a sinner, saved by grace.

Reflecting on the reading:

1. *How do you identify yourself? Do you ever feel less than?*

2. *How can you see yourself how God sees you, how He created you?*

3. *What three things can you pray over this week to help you find your worth in Jesus Christ?*

Weekly readings:
Jeremiah 1:4-5, 17-19; Psalm 71:1-6, 15-17; 1 Corinthians 12:31--13:13; Luke 4:21-30

Hope Beyond Healing

-THERESA BLACKSTONE

I thank you, Lord, with all my heart; in the presence of the angels to you I sing.

PSALM 138:1

In today's psalm, the psalmist cries out to God and knows that God will remain faithful to the end. He sings thanks and praise for the faithfulness of God even in the dark times, in danger, fear, suffering and sorrow. I love the psalmist's confidence in the goodness of God despite all earthly travails. Confidence in God's promise of heaven *is hope,* and it is that hope that sustains us even through the trials of our earthly pilgrimage.

In early October, my husband and I listened in shock and grief to the doctor's suspected diagnosis for our baby, then twenty weeks old *in utero.* Her initial concerns were confirmed in December and the prognosis was grim: if our daughter survived to birth, she would likely not live long.

The anguish and uncertainty of those months before Monica's birth were a burden in my soul like no other. I was helpless to secure the future of the fragile life that I had been sustaining inside me. I struggled to understand why God would bless us with a child only to call her home so soon afterward. Despite my sorrow and confusion, by the grace of God, I was spared a crisis of faith. I never felt abandoned by God. I never doubted His goodness. But I wondered how He would manifest it in this heart-wrenching and apparently hopeless situation.

I prayed constantly for Monica but struggled to know exactly how to pray for her healing. I desperately wanted to have the kind of zealous faith that would allow me to lay my hands on my large belly, declare, "By the power of God, the Divine Healer, you are healed!" and know without a doubt that God had worked that miracle. Instead, my steadfast prayer was, "Lord, I beg for the complete and total healing of Monica, but everything according to Your will and purpose, for our good and Your glory." Because there was always a little voice deep inside me that said, *He might not.* He might not heal her.

As it grew closer to the time of Monica's birth and her condition remained unchanged, praying for a miracle started to feel like a formality. I had little hope left that that particular prayer would be answered, but continued to ask for the miracle and also that God would be glorified whatever the outcome. A week before her birth, a friend pulled me aside and related an experience she had while praying before the Blessed Sacrament. She had been praying for Monica, begging God for a miracle, when she heard God say, "Monica *is* the miracle."

That shook me to the core. If my prayer for a miracle had already been granted, then whatever came next was surely a continued expression of God's goodness! Instead of weighty uncertainty, I began to feel more hopeful expectation and peace. The desire for God to be glorified in all circumstances became stronger in my heart. I continued to pray for her healing but knew with certainty that God was already manifesting His goodness through Monica, whether she survived one day or one hundred years. Her *life*, her story, not her health, was the miracle.

Ultimately, her earthly life was short; she returned home to our Heavenly Father only two days after her birth. But I know from countless messages and conversations that a great many people experienced a conversion or a renewed hope of heaven because of Monica's miraculous life and the grace of God.

She renewed *my* hope of Heaven! The promise of joining Monica in eternity, and spending forever-after praising God for His goodness, is a hope that fortifies this pilgrim!

Reflecting on the reading:

1. *When have you experienced unbearable loss in your life?*
2. *How do you seek God's perspective of healing in this world of pain and death?*
3. *How can we begin to view our pain and suffering as miracles?*

Weekly readings: Isaiah 6:1-2a, 3-8; Psalm 138:1-8; 1 Corinthians 15:1-11; Luke 5:1-11

The Dormancy of Hope

-MELODY LYONS

Blessed are those who trust in the Lord; the Lord will be their trust. They are like a tree planted beside the waters that stretches out its roots to the stream: It does not fear heat when it comes, its leaves stay green; In the year of drought it shows no distress, but still produces fruit.

JEREMIAH 17:7-8

As a native of Northeast Ohio, I understand the deep struggle of a soul during the dormancy of February sunshine. Christmas has long passed and the cold and dark days weigh heavily on a people who long for warmth of a new season. My thoughts invariably turn inward and I tend to lose a sense of the sun, of proper direction... of hope. It is an insomnia season when all the elements converge and conspire against the coveted commodity called sleep, deep sleep.

I met a mom one February whose struggles looked a lot like mine and when she shared a little piece of her grief, my own heart broke. I lay awake all night writing letters to her in my mind. She wanted to know if we moms can hope to repair the damage we have done to our own households over the years. *Tell me we can!* she begged. *Tell me we can go back and reverse what we have done.* I whispered a tiny and sad *no* inside my head and the discomfort of twenty-one years of mothering failures flooded into my mind and stomach.

Deep in February gloom, I went down, down into the ugliest thoughts. I let the projector reel of time run in my mind. I cringed. And I answered. *No. You can't go back.* You can't repair all the damage. The scars will stay - some for a little while and some for a lifetime. The people in our households are formed under our love, and also our sin. My children may spend the rest of their lives healing from and forgiving me the consequences of my sins. My laziness. My impatience. My lack of charity. My selfishness.

For years, I directed much of my motherly frustration against others who hurt my children. *Why, Lord, do You allow people to choose evil? To choose sin? To hurt my children?* And then the day came when I raised my hands and yelled:

Why, Lord, have You allowed ME to wound my children? I couldn't understand in the moment that His perfection only comes in our weakness. In the cloud of my pride, the grace of God was obscured. All that was visible to me was my failure.

The great confidence of my early motherhood faded as I saw my failures mirrored to me in the lives of my growing kids. To stay rooted like a tree and green even in the heat, I read the lives of the saints and recognized the weakness of their humanity, their allergies, their tempers, their errors, their conflicts. I saw that I had been placing confidence in the creation instead of the Creator and I fell into a consolation of humility. My pride lay stretched out and broken on the living room rug every single day. Mary, Mother of Sorrows became an ally for the first time. And the cross of motherhood, once a lovely but distant mystery, nestled itself deeply in my heart. My greatest consolation was the abiding love of God, who made Himself very present to me, even as my broken heart bled out into every area of my life.

Why does He allow this kind of stripping of soul? Perhaps because once we know that we are absolutely nothing without Him, we might finally learn how to pray and truly seek Him. We will not be uprooted. We will not be deceived by the flesh.

There simply is no answer apart from the Cross. Jesus is the Savior and *I am not Jesus.* In our journey toward sanctity, we eventually must realize that either He will be the answer to the heartache of our homes... or no one will.

We must learn how to walk again in hope and to relearn what it means to be alive as a child of God. I think that is the gift of a dormant February; we learn the gift of being rooted in Christ and Christ alone. Truly, it can be a terrifically painful and ongoing conversion, but also a moment of unparalleled joy. Thanks be to God.

Reflecting on the reading:

1. *Do your parenting failures replay in the reel of your mind?*
2. *How can you forgive yourself and seek God's grace for your own failures?*
3. *How can you learn how to walk again in hope and to live fully as a child of God?*

Weekly readings: Jeremiah 17:5-8; Psalm 1:1-4, 6; 1 Corinthians 15:12, 16-20; Luke 6:17, 20-26

February 24, 2019 (7th Sunday in Ordinary Time)

Speeding Tickets and Birthdays

-DR. PHIL KIM

Merciful and gracious is the Lord, slow to anger, abounding in mercy.

PSALM 103:8

In west Philadelphia, I was born and raised. Yes, the same as the Fresh Prince of Bel-Air. Admit it, you are now humming the song. Sorry. As the youngest child of South Korean immigrant parents, I had the "opportunity" to work for free at all of my parents' businesses. I worked in various versions of our family's convenience stores and sandwich shops. We even had a lunch truck that tried to capitalize on the foot traffic of business professionals and the local colleges and universities in the Philly area.

I was never allowed to drive the lunch truck, but I was still a pretty good driver. I think the reason is, I started driving well before the legal age of 16. As the first to emigrate from Korea, all of my dad's extended family members came through to live in our house for a couple of months or years as they got their footing underneath them in America. There were always random cars in the driveway. And not only did people in my family not lock their doors, they also left their keys in the car so as not to lose them. Brilliant!

As a young teen, I would always volunteer to go do chores for my aunts and uncles. Oh, you need some milk to go with that recipe? I'll be right back! Before anyone knew what was going on, I'd jump into one of their cars in our driveway and speed off to 7-11 to get a gallon of milk. What could they say? They didn't have a license either!

The first time I got a ticket, I was shocked. Not because I was pulled over, but in my 2+ years of driving before the legal age, I never came close to a traffic violation or infraction. I thought driving was so simple. The year I turned 16, and every year for the next five years, I got pulled over for speeding. To further kick me in the teeth, it was almost always on or around my birthday (August 2nd). It became a notorious birthday tradition for me. If I could make it past August without a ticket, I was safe for the next 11.5 months.

It took me a good five years to realize that I should probably slow down and obey the speed limit.

Fast forward to today and I've been ticket free for the past two decades! No, please don't clap. I'm only doing what I'm supposed to be doing. But thank you.

That is, until this past year.

This past year, I was pulled over for speeding. And if my father were still responsible for paying these tickets, I would want the officers to put me in jail for my protection.

I will say, being in my 40s, something has changed. I don't know if it's because I'm now driving a minivan with a rooftop carrier and a child seat or I just look like I've paid my life's worth of tickets already, but in this incident I received a firm warning from the officer to be more mindful as I drive in local areas.

I profusely thanked the officer for his leniency and assured him I would pay more attention as I drove. Driving home that day, I saw each and every speed limit sign.

I was so grateful for the warning because I was clearly in the wrong. But I was given mercy. I did not obey the rules and it would have been just for the police officer to enforce the law.

The same is true of our daily walk with God's grace. Every day we have an opportunity to follow God's commands, and every day we fail in some way. And yet, God is full of compassion and longs to extend grace to us. And it's nothing we do that earns this grace; it's all because of His abounding love for us.

When we receive mercy from someone, it's not a reflection of who we are, it's a reflection of who they are. And when we forgive others as Christ forgave us, it's a reflection of the One who abounds in love.

Reflecting on the reading:

1. *How do you find hope in the midst of life's chaos?*

2. *How can you reflect on these three truths each day?*

   - *God is merciful and gracious- He longs to forgive you even when you don't deserve it.*

   - *He is slow to anger - God is patient and long-suffering with your sin.*

   - *He abounds in love – His love is overflowing for you.*

Weekly readings: 1 Samuel 26:2, 7-9, 12-13, 22-23; Psalm 103:1-4, 8, 10, 12-13; 1 Corinthians 15:45-49; Luke 6:27-38

Death is Swallowed up in Victory

-REBECCA DUSSAULT

My dear brothers and sisters, stand firm. Let nothing move you. Always give yourselves fully to the work of the Lord, because you know that your labor in the Lord is not in vain.

1 CORINTHIANS 15:58

I couldn't feel the kicking. It had been a few days since I felt alerted. At twenty-eight weeks I had gone from carrying a circus performer in my womb to a very quiet child--too quiet, in fact. I hastily called the midwife and scheduled myself into the local hospital that afternoon for a sonogram.

The sonogram was routine and the circus of activity ensued as I stared at the screen, concluding everything was just fine with our fifth child, but that was a cascading moment. From there we were rapidly sent to larger and larger hospitals until our ticket was punched all the way from Colorado to Boston Children's Hospital in a few short weeks.

Our hearts wandered aimlessly, trying to understand our new reality of raising a baby with HLHS (hypo-plastic left heart syndrome). Needing three open-heart surgeries, where would this child be born? What was the chance of a good and full life for him after literally re-plumbing his beating heart?

The reality weighed in and despite our eagerness to move ahead with the intra-uterine heart surgery in Boston, it was not to be. Once there, the doctors recognized my signs of early labor and concluded they could do nothing if our baby were born there, at that stage, too small for surgery. I was most certainly going to go into labor if they proceeded with the surgery.

So we were back on the airplane, heading home, crumpled and in disbelief. We landed in Denver despite having labored silently on the direct flight. We had to get nearer to our other four children and I sent my husband back home to tend to them, all in the throes of horrible whooping cough.

It wasn't pleasant. It wasn't beautiful. It wasn't understandable, but somehow it was right. Through it all, we kept that peace the world cannot give because we'd seen hurdles before in life and had jumped them as a couple, as a family, secure in the hope of our faith. So it was right.

We asked death where was its sting. We asked death where was its victory. We faced the probable passing of our precious little child with faith, hope and peace that can only come from God.

The doctors eventually concluded that our baby would need to be born weighing a minimum of three pounds-three ounces. Finally, we had a marker to meet. I cannot say we had much hope that we would meet that marker because for five weeks, our baby's growth had stalled at two pounds-eight ounces. Nevertheless, we prayed for God's will, be it to increase the size of our baby rapidly, readying our child to be a fighter, or to call our child heavenward and give him the crown of life.

Remarkably, after two weeks of couch surfing in the city with friends and family, my husband's work brought him back to town. We went to our routine fetal echo together, only to conclude our precious baby was possibly improving and we needed to move the family forward on relocating. My husband headed home to make that happen.

Shortly after that good news, however, I went into full-blown labor and my husband had to turn around and hurry back to me. Our adorable young son, Joseph, was born into our hands shortly after we arrived at the hospital. He was accompanied by the prayers of a holy Byzantine priest who prayed the Psalms unceasingly for two hours until little Joseph's passing, also granting him an emergent Baptism.

With the passing of our precious Joseph on my chest, death indeed had been clothed with immortality (1 Corinthians 15:54). No parent is made naturally strong enough to bury their own child, unless these words are taken to heart: "My dear brothers and sisters, stand firm. Let nothing move you. Always give yourselves fully to the work of the Lord, because you know that your labor in the Lord is not in vain" (1 Corinthians 15:58).

And today and forevermore, death is swallowed up in victory. Praise be to God.

Reflecting on the reading:

1. How can you seek God in the midst of loss?

2. How can you pray this week for those who have lost a child?

3. How can you shine the hope of Christ into the lives of those around you who are in the midst of their own loss?

Weekly readings: Sirach 27:4-7; Psalm 92:2-3, 13-16; 1 Corinthians 15:54-58; Luke 6:39-45

A Pain that No One Sees

-DR. ANGELA MILLER

But when you pray, go to your inner room, close the door, and pray to your Father in secret.
And your Father who sees in secret will repay you.

MATTHEW 6:6

All of us experience pain. Some pain brings visual scars, physical reminders of what we have experienced. There are other types of pain though. Pain that lurks and lingers. Pain that drains the color from our days and clouds our view of the Son. Pain that seems to fill every cell of our body, but somehow remains invisible. A pain that no one sees.

When I was eighteen, I was diagnosed with polycystic ovary syndrome (PCOS), and was told that I would most likely not be able to have children. Then in 2015, I was excited to learn that we were expecting our fourth child. We were thrilled that their predictions had been wrong. I had three beautiful children through three uneventful pregnancies. I had no reason to believe anything would be different this time. That is, until the day I found myself sitting in the stark coldness of an emergency room listening to a faraway voice tell me that my baby was gone.

In that moment, a depth of grief and brokenness that far surpassed anything I had ever known washed over me. I named our child John Marie. Like John the Baptist, I cried out in my wilderness. I held on to the image of Mary at the foot of the cross and was saddened as the world moved on even when I didn't.

Soon after that, we were expecting again. Fear settled in where unbridled joy had once lived. Yet we still anticipated, still planned. We held on to our mustard seed and we hoped. In June, our child, Regina Luke, went home to be with the Lord. I was numb. Disbelief robbed me of clarity. *Salve Regina* became my prayer. Heal me, Divine Physician, was my plea. It all seemed like a cruel joke.

We are blessed to live in a vibrant, faith-filled community. I watched many friends progress in their pregnancies and come home with beautiful babies. Blessings indeed, but salt in a wound not yet healed. There was so much emptiness, so many questions as I blamed myself. So many awkward moments as I tried to figure out how to answer, "How many children do you have?" The darkness threatened to extinguish the Light.

It's always been funny to me that just when you think you can't possibly find any more strength to take another step, God equips you to go a little further. For me, this happened as we walked this path of loss two more times that year. By the time we lost Isaac Grace in November, I was different. I had been in my desert long enough and there was nothing left for me to do but surrender. Like Abraham, I laid my child at the feet of God and prayed for the grace to do what He asked of me. On December 23, I used that grace when I heard His call once more and I learned that little Samuel Guadalupe was gone.

Matthew 6 is read every year in preparation for Lent. I always heard in it an admonition about sin and pride and the importance of rooting out those things from our lives that separate us from God. While I still recognize that message, what I lived in 2015 taught me something that changed forever how I will hear these verses. My pain separated me from God. It became a wall I could not get past on my own. It was a pain no one could see. No one, that is, but God. My Father, who sees in secret, always saw. Always heard. Never forgot. Never abandoned me. When I allowed Him to work, He planted so many seeds. He didn't remove all my pain, but He showed me how to use it. He tended the garden of my heart, a garden I didn't plant, and through Him it is beautiful.

All of us experience pain. Some pain is visible and some is invisible. But take heart, God sees it all. God wants to heal your pain. He sees you. He loves you. He knows what you need. This Lent, allow the God of all healing into your dark, secret places of pain and rise with Christ this Easter.

Reflecting on the reading:

1. *How can both visible and invisible pain negatively impact your life?*

2. *Are you carrying invisible pain in your soul?*

3. *How can you allow the God of all healing to help you rise with Christ this Easter?*

Ash Wednesday readings: Joel 2:12-18; Psalm 51:3-6ab, 12-14, 17; 2 Corinthians 5:20-6:2; Matthew 6:1-6, 16-18

Even in this
-KATE MEDINA

..for, if you confess with your mouth that Jesus is Lord and believe in your heart that
God raised him from the dead, you will be saved.
ROMANS 10:9

The celebration began as our good friends arrived home from halfway around the globe. Travel-weary, but overjoyed as their family multiplied through adoption in both love and chaos. We could see this beautiful redemption story stretching out before us. Their journey evidenced our good and faithful God and buoyed our hope in all things made new.

Only a few months later, news of her diagnosis knocked us back on our heels. Apathetic numbers rapidly connected. Stage four. She's barely in her thirties...with two babies...maybe less than one year? And just like that, fear colored everything.

Sometimes life hands you a story you don't want to tell. The kind that deconstructs everything you once held close and true. It's a daily re-education, slogging through the agonizing plot line. You search hard and angry through devastating facts to grasp for purpose in the appalling, only to find that sometimes this is just what life requires. And what can you do but reach for courage somewhere within your fractured heart?

The initial shock settled and everyday life continued, but we were helpless to change the unfolding of her story. Sifting through our faith to find purpose in the mess of it all, darkness had its way with us. We found ourselves relentlessly questioning, and desperately needing God all at once. Our hearts crumbled and swelled with the grace-filled words our dear friend crafted to tell this unwelcome narrative, and I am convinced there is no greater beauty than tear-stained hallelujahs.

Palms up in surrender, heart clutching both life and loss, and lips loose with praise, her posture told all. It reverberated "Thy kingdom come." Somehow, within the repulsive ruins, she understood that it was never about her kingdom anyway. And it was this hope-filled knowledge that allowed her to push fear aside with every defiant hallelujah.

It. Was. Breathtaking.

There are a thousand furious questions and some serious fist shaking for a lot of us. Truthfully, no one escapes the human experience without some degree of heartbreak. Although we are instructed to pick up our crosses, not our comfort, suffering can lead us to doubt, discouragement and disbelief. So, we must answer again and again.

"Who do you say I am?" (Mark 8:29)

Jesus aimed the question at Peter, whose response flickered with brilliance, "You are the Christ, the Messiah." Yes, at that moment, Peter knew the depth of it. How we answer this question in the deep of our despair will determine how we overcome the wreckage this side of heaven.

Sometimes we misunderstand this living to be all about us, our storyline and our desired outcomes. Bitterness can envelope all the side plots we never saw coming, as affliction shreds our well-penned scripts. How easy to confuse our kingdom with His.

It was a hard but holy rewrite for my friend. Joy and sorrow, faith and fear, understanding and mystery, scribbled together meticulously. She chose to believe that His goodness, His love, and His grace could be found in both light and darkness. And she trusted God through all of it, as her steadfast answer remained, "Even in this, You are the Messiah." And it was a most beautiful redemption story indeed.

Reflecting on the reading:

1. *When did life feel like wreckage to you?*
2. *How do joy and sorrow, faith and fear inhabit our hearts at the same time?*
3. *How can you trust God even in this?*

Weekly readings: Deuteronomy 26:4-10; Psalm 91:1-2, 10-15; Romans 10:8-13; Luke 4:1-13

Whispering His Name

-MARIA WALTHER

I believe I shall see the Lord's goodness in the land of the living. Wait for the Lord, take courage; be stouthearted, wait for the Lord!

PSALM 27:13-14

It's easy to have hope, easy to choose joy, in the moments when everything is going beautifully in our lives. In an instant, however, our world can be turned upside down, and it is what we choose to do in those moments, who we choose to cling to and turn to, that is our saving grace.

Years back, my husband and I had two children and miscarried a precious soul on Christmas day. Then we found ourselves pregnant again. I wasn't the wife and mother I thought I would be, and I was scared. But I knew that the Lord must have a beautiful plan for our lives. However, at a routine visit when I was seven and a half months pregnant, the nurse could not find our daughter's heartbeat. As I looked at the ultrasound and saw a still, silent heart, all I could think, all I could say, all I could whisper was "Jesus...Jesus...Jesus."

The Lord heard me. I couldn't pray or say anything other than His name, but I called upon His name and He heard me. I didn't understand why this was happening. I couldn't comprehend what the next days would hold. It was indescribable. We lost Moriah Faith on February 2, 2005. We chose her name from the book of Genesis, chapter 22, when Abraham is called to the land of Moriah, and his faith saves Isaac. Through this very dark time in our lives, Jesus was with me, walking beside me. I was not afraid. Jesus was carrying us through the valley, helping us bear this cross. I also knew that we would not be in the valley forever, and I longed for brighter days.

It wasn't long before the Lord carried us up to the highest mountain. We felt the Lord was calling us to trust in Him and to have faith that all would be well. It was the hardest and greatest sacrifice that we have been asked to make. The Lord, in His goodness and mercy, blessed us with Helena Mercy exactly a year to the day that we lost Moriah. Then on February 2, 2008, we welcomed Gemma Charity. The Lord didn't ask us to wait very long to see the blessings that He had for us.

I know that this isn't always how things work out, but what I also know is that we have a loving Father who calls us to Him. He longs for us to call His name. He longs for us to reach out to Him and allow ourselves to be carried.

We look at our six precious children here on earth (we have had two boys since our girls), and are thankful for the beautiful children waiting for us in Heaven. When I think of the day that we lost Moriah, I can't comprehend how we made it through. I cannot imagine being asked to carry that cross again.

However, I do know that it was by His grace that we made it through. I do know that by His grace you can carry any cross that is placed before you. It won't be easy. It's not meant to be easy. But we have this light. We have this hope. We have no need to be afraid. He has carried us before, and He will carry us again.

When we call upon His name, He not only hears us, but He is merciful and answers us. It might not be immediately. It might not be in a loud booming voice. But in the quiet whispers, we can hear His voice answer our prayers. He isn't going to ask us to face these valleys alone, for He will walk with us.

Will we only praise the name of Jesus when all is good? Or will we seek Him, run to Him, know Him through every valley and mountain in this life? And when we call upon the name of the Lord, we can know that sometimes, the most beautiful prayers are often those found when we simply whisper the name of Jesus.

Reflecting on the reading:

1. Have you experienced a deep dark valley in this life?

2. Have you experienced the beautiful mountaintop of success, joy and happiness?

3. How can you continue to whisper the name of Jesus through every mountain and valley you walk?

Weekly readings: Genesis 15:5-12, 17-18; Psalm 27:1, 7-9, 13-14; Philippians 3:17-4:1; Luke 9:28b-36

Standing Firm

-GAIL KNARR

Therefore, whoever thinks he is standing secure should take care not to fall.
1 CORINTHIANS 10:12

As a lifelong rule-follower, I always thought that my "standing firm" was a good thing. I mean, the rules were God's rules, and as long as I obeyed His rules (and tried to enforce them with my younger siblings), everything was going to be great in my life. Unfortunately, that mindset led to me being somewhat judgmental. Junior high and high school were tough - friends started experimenting with smoking, drinking, drugs, sex. Those were all against my rules, and I was sure God didn't approve, either! Anyone who defied the rules on which I was standing firm became flawed in my eyes. Mentally, I would toss them out of my perfect little "rule box."

Fast forward to young adulthood. Still believing I was standing firm on my "rules," and therefore right in all I did and believed, I found myself mentally judging many people in my life. Coworkers who were living with a significant other, young women who got pregnant out of wedlock, college classmates who drank too much at a party on the (dry) campus of my small Christian college. All were subject to my silent judgment, and my feeling that I was clearly better than them.

Fast forward again to my forties. By then I had begun to realize that people make mistakes and it doesn't make them "bad" or unworthy of God's love. He loves me, He loves you. He loves them. In my forties, I began to understand forgiveness on a more mature level, having experienced the power of forgiveness firsthand. And yet I still had my judgmental tendencies, still felt in my mind that I was better than a lot of these people because I hadn't done some of the terrible things they had done. It was as if I believed God loved me more because I was better than them, because I had followed the "rules."

And then my world turned upside down. My rule-following husband was arrested. He had been battling an addiction to pornography for close to thirty years and had been able to keep it quite well hidden, even from me. I had known about his issues with pornography prior to our marriage, but I thought he had overcome this addiction. I had no idea that it continued and that it had escalated. Over the next few months, my husband faced job loss, court hearings, shame and embarrassment in the community and our church as rumors circulated.

One morning, we went together to the County Department of Health to be tested for HIV and other STDs. I can honestly say it was the most humiliating experience of my life. I was, after all, a rule follower. How could this be happening to us? I sat in the waiting room looking around at the others there, mentally judging them: "Does she even know who the father of her baby is?" "He's probably high right now," "How could she show her face in public looking like that?"

And then it happened. God spoke to me, saying, "You're here too." In that instant, in a quiet whisper from God, it all became very clear - I had been "standing firm" for so long, judging everyone around me for so many years, and now I was the one who had fallen. So I took a deep breath, whispered a soft prayer, and began to look at the people in that waiting room beside me through God's eyes. I began to pray for them, that he might find a much needed job, that she had help raising her baby, and that he was able to get help and get off of drugs.

Through journeying through a very dark place in my life, God gave me new eyes. I had been standing firm on the rules, and forgetting that what I needed to stand firm on was God, His love, His grace, His sacrifice for us. On that day in the waiting room, I began to see people as God sees them, and I know that I am not called to judge, rather I am called to love. Through loving others, I might even shine the light of hope, the light of Jesus, into someone's life.

Reflecting on the reading:

1. Have you ever caught yourself judging someone by the way they looked or by sin in their life?

2. Have you ever felt judged by others? How did that feel?

3. How can you be sure you are standing on the Rock, Jesus Christ?

Weekly readings: Exodus 3:1-8a, 13-15; Psalm 103:1-4, 6-8, 11;
1 Corinthians 10:1-6, 10-12; Luke 13:1-9

A New Creation
-CHRISTINA NIETO

So whoever is in Christ is a new creation: the old things have passed away;
behold, new things have come.
2 CORINTHIANS 5:17

I have so often cried out to God, "What must you think of me?"

While trying to be a good wife and mother, I am aware of my responsibility to break my family's cycle of divorce, abuse and dysfunction. I ask God to heal my brokenness and I long to be closer to Him. I've always struggled with my relationship with God the Father because all I knew was an earthly father who was sick with alcoholism and abusive towards his family. His father was even worse than he was, and as a young child, I learned about trust and security from a man who exposed me to traumatic situations.

For years I battled bouts of anxiety and depression and eventually sought treatment after the death of my mother from breast cancer. I was twenty-three years old. During my time in treatment, I was not practicing my faith. I was baptized Catholic as an infant, and church was sprinkled into my youth but never held the central focus. Then one day, God called me into a church and back to the faith I had been baptized into. God showed me how He forgives us our trespasses through the gift of reconciliation.

It's been about ten years now that I have been daily living my faith and have completely surrendered to the love of God the Father. I am constantly aware of my own inner struggles and the work it takes to heal as I re-learn appropriate thoughts, skills and behaviors. I attempt to surround myself with holy relationships and learn to love through the eyes of Christ.

It is difficult some days to not fall back into old patterns. My truth of not growing up with a good example of marriage and family has challenged me to work harder. I often see my own failures and know that the enemy wants me to focus on them. I turn to our Lord in those times. I ask Him to show me that I am healing on this journey, I am doing His will, and I am making my Father in heaven proud.

As my relationship with God the Father developed and I began to feel worthy and renewed in His spirit, I was blessed to go on retreat with an amazing community of women. I was led into some deep examination of all the grief in my life. This was hard work and, for lack of a better word, quite depressing to see all the stuff I had lived through. But God remained faithful and He assured me I had survived those years.

I returned home to my beautiful children and supportive husband who make me laugh even when I don't always feel like laughing. (My family is my life, and my focus is taking care of them and making sure Christ is the center of our lives.) A few days later, I received an email from a hospital system I had used years ago. I had never opened any communication about checking my records from them because I hadn't been seen there in years. But this time something drew me to open it and review my records. There, from years ago, was my mental health diagnosis, which I had never seen. I was diagnosed with histrionic personality disorder, and even typing this I feel such a stigma with the word "disorder." Today I may exhibit some tendencies, but I am definitely not the person I was when I was suffering, when I was in my darkest days of mental illness.

God left the ninety-nine to find me. He welcomed me home with open arms and the fattened calf. God showed me who I was so that I could see who I am now "in Him." For years I ignored looking at those records and did not give it a second thought until now. I realize how God strengthened me and gave me the wisdom to see all He has done for me.

I am a new creation. I am in Christ, and He is in me, making all things new. The old has gone, the new is here, both in my faith and in my life.

Reflecting on the reading:

1. *Think of a time in your life when you chose to break a bad habit and become new in Christ.*

2. *How can you be an ambassador for Christ through your experiences as you encounter others?*

3. *How can we reconcile with one another and support those suffering with mental illness?*

Weekly readings: Joshua 5:9a, 10-12; Psalm 34:2-7; 2 Corinthians 5:17-21; Luke 15:1-3, 11-32

Thanks, Dad

-HANNAH BERG

See, I am doing something new! Now it springs forth, do you not perceive it?
In the wilderness I make a way, in the wasteland, rivers.
ISAIAH 43:19

I have always felt a sense of peace walking in the woods. I grew up on a farm surrounded by our own little woods. As a child, I loved spending time out there. My dad would take my siblings and me out to the woods to hunt for wild mushrooms. We would get our shoes on, grab our plastic grocery bags and run off to the woods, usually arguing about who would find the most mushrooms.

After we had hunted until our bags were full, we would turn around and look to Dad to find our way home again, back through the trees and over the hills to our little farmhouse in the valley. Every single time we would look to my dad to lead us back, he would glance around and then turn back to us with a scared look on his face, saying, "Girls, I think we're lost!"

My sister and I, believing every word he said, would start to wonder if we would ever find our way back home! We looked up at the tall, scary trees and let the fear of the unknown creep up on us. Seeing the fear on our little faces, my dad would reassure us. "It's okay," he would say. "We'll be fine. Hannah, you have to find our way back now."

He would turn to me since I was two years older than my sister. So as the oldest, I would go to the front of our little woods-walking parade and start to try and figure out our way back home. With every turn I made, I could hear my dad call out behind me, "Good job, just keep going! Just find the path!" After a while, I would start to see the path that we needed to get home. My sister and I would suddenly run on the path, out of the woods until we could see our little farmhouse. We would be giggling and talking the whole way back about how we were almost lost in the wilderness forever, but together we found our way home.

I've never asked my dad why he used to make me find our way back home. Maybe it was just for his own amusement, since he knew exactly where to go the whole time. Maybe it was just to instill confidence in me, or maybe just to kill time. But I don't think he could have imagined how much it would impact my adult life and how I look to those little lessons as a way to get through any wilderness I find myself in today.

Right now, my life really feels like a big forest of tall, scary trees. I'm a recent college graduate, living in a new place in a new city, trying to make new friends all while starting graduate school. Tall trees are everywhere I look. It's like I'm back in those woods with my dad and I don't know where to turn. Except this time, I'm all alone.

Or so I thought.

I'm still learning that God is bigger than even the biggest trees I face. And even when I feel overwhelmed and let my anxiety get the best of me, He is right there behind me. "It's okay," God says. "Just keep walking; find My path."

The Lord declares that He is "making a way in the wilderness and streams in the wasteland (Isaiah 43:19b). He has an aerial view of my wilderness and even when I can't see His path clearly, He can. He can see your path, too.

He went ahead of us and made sure our paths lead to greater things than we could ever imagine. We just have to be still enough to listen to His quiet encouragement leading us along the way. Even when we feel alone, He is right there with us. No matter how intimidating our wilderness seems.

I have always felt a sense of peace walking in the woods. I learned to rely on my dad and trust his encouragement to find the path.

Now, as an adult, I am finding my way through this life, relying on God, and trusting in His voice as He guides my steps.

Thanks, Dad.

Reflecting on the reading:

1. What "trees" in your life are making you feel lost today?

2. How can you be still, and listen for God's voice to guide you to His path?

3. How can your prayer life reflect your trust in His plan for your life?

Weekly readings: Isaiah 43:16-21; Psalm 126:1-6; Philippians 3:8-14; John 8:1-11

Rich in What Matters to God

-LISA HENDEY

But God said to him, "You fool, this night your life will be demanded of you; and the things
you have prepared, to whom will they belong?" Thus will it be for the one who stores up
treasure for himself but is not rich in what matters to God.

LUKE 12:20-21

By all outward appearances, Greg and I "had it all." The big suburban house with a pool and guest area to welcome visiting family and friends. The job for him that paid well, provided career satisfaction and garnered respect. The parish that felt like home and was filled with friends.

We daydreamed about living out the rest of our working years in comfort, awaiting those golden years when a paid-off mortgage would surely mean the "good life" for us and our extended family.

Then Greg was offered his dream job and suddenly our well-laid plans were shaken and swirled like the glitter in a snow globe. Accepting this wonderful opportunity would mean moving from suburbia into a far smaller urban abode, getting rid of two-thirds of our possessions, saying goodbye to friends, and venturing into the unknown.

During our period of prayerfully discerning our possible relocation, I had to leave for the Philippines. We knew his job offer letter was coming soon and that a decision was at hand. We committed to pray together, despite the miles that separated us, that we could give God our "yes" to His will for our lives, wherever that might lead us.

I landed in Manila and had the great joy of visiting little Jackilyn and her family. Our family had connected with Jackilyn's through a sponsorship opportunity with Unbound. With a translator in tow, my trip to their urban home involved commuting in a bus, a "jeepney" and even a motorcycle sidecar. When I arrived, I found this precious little elementary schoolgirl, her sisters and her parents standing proudly near a home that is approximately the size of some backyard garden sheds in the United States.

Jackilyn's mom and dad welcomed me inside for a meal and fellowship and we passed the most beautiful day sharing stories, playing games, and laughing. Their "tiny" house was large enough to contain and multiply the joy we all felt in being together. I was reminded that "home" is not a building, but rather a sense of belonging.

In today's scripture, Luke recounts Jesus' telling of the parable of the rich fool. The wealthy farmer whose bumper crop had produced an abundant harvest determined to build larger barns to accommodate his newfound bounty. He was already anticipating the many years when he could "rest, eat, drink, be merry!" Nowhere in the passage do we read of the fool sharing his wealth with those in need. Nowhere do we find him looking to take even a portion of his excess to serve others.

In that parable, as so often happens in our lives, God reminded the fool that wealth and ultimate security are not our end goal, and he came to a different end, one very different from the good life he'd planned. A fully funded retirement account is not a bad thing, but when we focus solely on material wealth without pursuing spiritual security or thinking of the needs of others, we miss the mark of what matters most.

Not long after my time with Jackilyn's family, Greg was offered, and accepted, his new role. My "decluttering" and downsizing became a full-time occupation as family treasures were gifted or donated. We moved four hours south into that whole new world, a new "mission territory" of sorts. Our new (to us!) home, built in 1937, is not quite as tiny as Jackilyn's but has taught me to continually strive to overcome my packrat tendencies. We now open our hearth to friends and neighbors without apologizing for what we lack, but rather with a desire to share, to welcome, and to love. Jackilyn's very "rich" family helped me prioritize this next phase of our family's life, where our greatest aspiration at this point is to be "rich in what matters most to God."

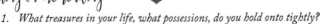

Reflecting on the reading:

1. *What treasures in your life, what possessions, do you hold onto tightly?*

2. *How can you re-focus your life to treasure things in heaven?*

3. *How can you view your family as being rich in what matters most to God?*

Weekly readings: Luke 19:28–40; Isaiah 50:4–7; Psalm 22:8–9, 17–20, 23–24;
Philippians 2:6–11; Luke 22:14–23:56

God's Grace Sets us Free

-BEN WALTHER

Tell the whole community of Israel: On the tenth of this month every family must procure for itself a lamb, one apiece for each household…They will take some of its blood and apply it to the two doorposts and the lintel of the houses in which they eat it.

EXODUS 12:3; 7

On this day, Holy Thursday, Christians everywhere remember the redemptive work of our Savior. The Catholic mass today begins with a reading from Exodus Chapter 12, recalling one of the most dramatic events of our salvation history: the Passover.

In doing battle with the gods of Egypt, the God of Israel bared His arm and put His strength on full display, sending plague upon plague to break the will of obstinate Pharoah. With every plague, God revealed His power over the Egyptian gods. Finally, to prove He is the author of life and death, He promised to send the Angel of Death through Egypt, striking down every firstborn in the land. The Israelites could only save their firstborn by spreading the blood of an unblemished lamb on the doorposts of their homes.

The blood of the lamb was their promise of loyalty and trust in God, and was their only hope for liberation. In giving explicit instructions for the Passover, God foreshadows the holy events of Jesus' Passion, death, and resurrection - the events we celebrate over the next few days.

When I was in high school, I was in the middle of a battle myself. My father gave up on our family, and we were left reeling from the shock of abandonment. After some time had passed, I became numb to the presence of God in my life. Much like the Israelites who had lived for several generations in Egypt, I dismissed God and began making plans for my own life without considering what our Heavenly Father had planned for me.

For a time, I believed that I would be doomed to repeat the mistakes my father made: marital infidelity and an over-commitment to career. I was not a great student during this time, and could not grasp a vision for what I thought my life should be. My hope was gone.

As my mother's grieving began to wane, she attended her prayer groups more vigorously. Her friends rallied around her, and she found much strength. Prophetically, she printed copies of scripture verses in large fonts, framed them, and set them around the house. One scripture verse I saw almost every day was Jeremiah 29:11: "For I know well the plans I have in mind for you... so as to give you a future of hope."

What I didn't know at sixteen is that God commanded Jeremiah to speak to the people of Israel in the middle of the Babylonian Exile, a time of great distress, suffering and hopelessness.

Why would God communicate Himself to a suffering people with so much confidence, eagerness and joy? Because He knows well the plan He has for us. God wants us to enjoy freedom and intimacy with Him. Seeing us in slavery, our Father wants to "execute judgment" on all our false gods as He did unto the gods of Egypt. Our gods might be fear, addiction, greed, lust or any other thing to which we give ourselves. God wants to show Himself mightier than these.

After attending a retreat for high school students with my youth group, I began to open up to the possibility of a "future of hope." God began to loosen the grip my false gods had on me. As I came to understand that Jesus is the true unblemished Lamb of God, I felt God calling me to daily mass where I could invite His sacred blood to cover the doorpost of my heart.

Every time I received communion, I could feel God leading me out of the bonds of slavery and into the light of liberation. Today, I am living in the "future full of hope" and there's more to come!

We should be encouraged on our journey with the Lord. In our struggle against sin and selfishness, let us remember that it is God's grace that sets us free, and His greatest desire is to do so! On this Holy Thursday, we choose to hope in God's promise, His power and His faithfulness.

Reflecting on the reading:

1. *How do you honor Holy Thursday in your family? Mass? Traditions?*

2. *Have you ever experienced doubt in God's plan for your life?*

3. *How can you pray your way through those times of doubt and trust in God's grace?*

Holy Thursday readings: Exodus 12:1-8, 11-14; Psalm 116:12-13, 15-16bc, 17-18; 1 Corinthians 11:23-26; John 13:1-15

The River

-EDEN GERBER

Be my rock of refuge, a stronghold to save me. For you are my rock and my fortress;
for your name's sake lead me and guide me.

PSALM 31:3b-4

Imagine you're walking along a fierce river after a tremendous storm. You see a puddle and try to avoid it, but slip and fall into the river anyway. The force of the water pulls you under. You surface, but just when you think you're going to be fine, you crash into a pile of boulders. It seems impossible to survive. Your vision starts to blur and the struggle to stay above the water is getting harder. Taking one last breath, you begin to sink into the deep water until, suddenly, a strong hand grasps yours and pulls you out. Your vision is better than before, and miraculously you are no longer soaked. A tall bearded man stands before you. He is glowing with love. In that moment, you recognize the face of your Savior.

After my sister, Evelyn, passed away three years ago, my life was like a raging river. I was swept away by the current because I wasn't strong enough to hold my ground. I was weak and angry, asking God why He would allow this to happen to Evelyn and to my family. I didn't get the answer right away.

Yet, I knew that God was still with me and I experienced moments of stillness and peace. Shortly after my sister died, my adorable baby brother Gabriel was born. We continued building our peaceful hobby farm that we had begun before my sister died. It was a new beginning for all of us. The next year, my mom gave birth to another baby, a beautiful little girl named Miriam, who makes me happy every time she smiles. I was overjoyed. It was like walking along the river after the storm--peaceful.

Then I came across another huge puddle. I started to show symptoms of depression at the age of ten. I tried to avoid talking to anyone about what was going on inside my head, but not talking made it worse. That's when I slipped on the puddle and plunged into the icy river yet again. I would not leave my room because of anxiety; I was too scared to go anywhere. My family tried their best for months to help me. Finally, thanks to a lot of support and prayer, I was able to leave the house long enough to start seeing a counselor. My therapist helped me a lot. It was like finding a new friend.

For a while, I was doing much better and I thought that everything was going to be ok. I was beginning to walk on firm ground again, and then our dog died suddenly. With yet another loss, reminding me of losing my sister so suddenly, I slipped once more and crashed into the river. I thought that I was sinking for good and nobody would be able to save me now. I wanted to give up on even trying to make progress.

But my Savior's hand plunged into the waters to save me yet again and I clung to Him. He was my refuge. I prayed and talked to Him about my anxiety, depression, grief, and the pressure of being a big sister. I put my trust in Him and talked to my family and best friend.

I am twelve years old now and I still sometimes struggle with that river. But I have hope in life and in our loving God. We all slip and fall into the river at some time in our lives. But when we do, we need to go to God and tell Him how we feel because He is always listening, crying and laughing along with us.

No matter how big the river may seem, don't be afraid to believe again. Stay strong and don't let other people make you feel weak. Remember how much God loves you and that you are beautiful in His eyes. And even if you fall into the river over and over, don't give up hope. Jesus loves you more than you could ever know. Just grab His strong hand and let Him pull you up into the light again.

Reflecting on the reading:

1. When have you experienced the river of pain and loss overtake your life?

2. In those moments, how can you reach for Jesus' hand and grasp it?

3. Are there people in your life who are suffering loss? How can you help them reach for Jesus' hand?

Good Friday readings: Isaiah 52:13-53:12; Psalm 31:2, 6, 12-13, 15-17, 25;
Hebrews 4:14-16; 5:7-9; John 18:1-19:42 (Passion Reading)

Little girl, arise!

-DR. CHAD GERBER

On the first day of the week, Mary of Magdala came to the tomb early in the morning, while it was still dark,[c] and saw the stone removed from the tomb.

JOHN 20:1

I've called many things in life "the worst thing in the world" - emptying the dishwasher, really long flights, and dental work to name a few. Such statements are obvious examples of gross exaggeration. Literally speaking, death is the worst thing in the world since it snatches from creation what is best – life itself.

On the afternoon of October 31, 2015, a life was plucked from my own family in the most unexpected of ways.

Two of my daughters were participating in a Halloween-themed piano recital. Eleven-year-old Evelyn was the second student to perform. After completing her short piece from memory, she stood and then appeared to begin her customary bow. It was not what it seemed. Evelyn continued downward until her entire body lay limp upon the floor, directly at the feet of her stunned siblings and friends. She was dead. Extensive testing would later reveal that she had been living with a rare genetic mutation capable of throwing the heart wildly (and often irreversibly) out of rhythm. We had no idea.

Burying your child is agonizing. It is also isolating. Throughout most of human history, however, burying loved ones was extremely common, though no less painful, as life expectancies were often half our own. These were certainly the cultural circumstances two millennia ago when a small band of men and women devoted themselves to a would-be Savior who called himself "The Life" and claimed He would conquer nothing less than death itself. He had even given His followers a preview of His plan by bringing several people back to life, including His old friend Lazarus and the daughter of Jairus, a local religious leader. But then, to their horror, He too was conquered by death. Or was he?

It was the first day of the workweek that crisp April morning; so early that it was still dark. Souvenir merchants had begun setting up tables near the temple, soldiers changed shifts outside the Praetorium, and several women carrying earthen jars made their way to Siloam to draw water for the day's cooking. Jerusalem was only beginning to wake up. But Peter and John were sprinting through her narrow streets. Mary of Magdala, out of breath from her own morning run, had just informed them that the tomb of Jesus was open and empty. They had to see for themselves.

So they ran, darting in and out of bewildered shopkeepers and curious soldiers, eventually passing through the eastern Gate of Gennath just as beams of daylight emerged above the notorious white limestone outcrop called The Skull. Sand and fragments of stone lodged in their sandals and pricked their soles. Yet they kept on running, oblivious to the pain because something else pricked their souls – thoughts of a giant stone purportedly removed the preceding night. Finally, John and then Peter reached the burial chamber and braced themselves against its rough-hewn entryway. Fighting for breath, they peered inside. They saw nobody. They saw no body. They saw only burial clothes neatly folded. This was clearly not the work of thieves. It was, as they had so fervently hoped, the work of God. Jesus had risen.

That morning, Peter, John, and Mary were still oppressed, ridiculed, and yes, mortal. Yet they had just witnessed something that would, in time, dramatically transform all things. That morning wasn't just the beginning of a new week; it was the beginning of a whole new creation – one immune to sin, suffering, and yes, death. What they saw therefore was "the best thing in the world" – ever. And that's no exaggeration, because the empty tomb signals the sure defeat of that literal "worst thing in the world."

As a grieving father, my soul is now fertile soil for this seminal truth. When I awake in the darkness of mourning, I may not run through the streets with anticipation, but my heart races. I may not peer into an empty tomb, but I see it with my mind's eye. I too am left breathless by the realization that Christ has indeed defeated death and, what's more, all who belong to Him will one day share in the spoils of His victory. For soon enough He will say to my precious Evelyn, as He did to Jairus's daughter centuries ago, "Talitha Koum."

Little girl, arise!

Reflecting on the reading:

1. Have you experienced tremendous loss in your life?

2. How do you mourn with hope? What does it mean to grieve as a Christian?

3. This week, what can you do to love and support someone who is grieving loss?

Weekly readings: Acts 10:34a, 37–43; Psalm 118:1-2, 16-17, 22-23; Colossians 3:1-4 or 1 Corinthians 5:6b-8; John 20:1-9 or Luke 24:1-12

I Do Believe

-BROOKE TAYLOR

"Put your finger here and see my hands, and bring your hand and put it into my side, and do not be unbelieving, but believe." Thomas answered and said to him, "My Lord and my God!"

JOHN 20:27-28

My youngest son Gus is prone to night terrors. One morning, I was abruptly awakened by the sound of his screams. He was frantic, almost inconsolable as I rushed into his bedroom, still half asleep. This time though, I noticed he was fully awake. In the darkness of the pre-dawn hours, he stood against his bedroom window with his palms gripping the glass crying out "MOM! COME BACK!"

As my husband backed out of the driveway for work, my four-year-old thought it was actually *me* heading out, leaving him alone. It took a moment for both of us to understand what was happening. As I reassured Gus that I was right there, his expression transformed from fear to relief. I could physically feel his breathing regulate as he relaxed into my arms, tears streaming down his face.

That moment has been such a lesson for me. Even now, several years later I recall that feeling as I meditate on the moment Jesus' appeared to Thomas and the disciples. The risen Lord is asking us to come near, melt into his embrace and trust that He is there. Despite what our eyes may tell us. Despite what we may sometimes feel.

The terror on Gus' face impacted me deeply because I recognized that same fear during specific times in my own life. A moment when your senses tell you something terrible is happening but your mind is unable to process or compute the reality.

When my daughter was diagnosed with severe institutional autism. The day we received news of my dad's terminal lung cancer. When my son had a stroke. The afternoon my best friend's daughter died.

As we grip the glass and look out the window to eternity, it may appear that our dreams, hopes and precious loved ones are leaving us behind. Life circumstances have the power to press us down to our knees, test everything we ever believed and sometimes tempt us to doubt all we know to be true.

In John 20:27-28, Thomas provides the evidence we need, proof beyond all reasonable doubt, that even in grief and unbelief, that Christ is in our midst.

A doubt that is voiced, a hope that is realized, a resurrection that is complete.

Thomas' profound confession of faith opens the door to a quantum portal, inviting us all to stand in his sandals and proclaim in ecstasy: "My Lord and my God!"

When my son realized that I had not left him after all, it gave him peace. A peace that was physically evident as his eyes locked on mine and his little body relaxed into my embrace.

How beautiful that our glorified Lord freely gives us His peace -"My peace I leave you."

May we embrace this gift like a baby belly-laughing, with our whole being, melting into His arms and exclaiming, "It is true! I do believe, Lord!"

Amen.

Reflecting on the reading:

1. Has there been a time in your life when you felt terror and panic?

2. Who did you turn to? Where did your comfort come from?

3. When you feel fear, how can you pray to seek the comfort of God's love?

Weekly readings: Acts 5:12-16; Psalm 118:2-4, 13-15, 22-24; Revelation 1:9-11a, 12-13, 17-19; John 20:19-31

H.O.P.E.
(Hand Over Problems Every Day)
-EMILY TAPPE

I praise you, Lord, for you raised me up and did not let my enemies rejoice over me.
PSALM 30:2

Hand over our problems to Jesus every day! Seems easy enough, right? I think most of us would say, "Wrong!" Any typical teenager, college student, mom, dad, full-time working adult, etc. encounters many problems throughout the day. God wants us to hand those problems over to Him and show Him our faith. He knows we will go through trials and hard times, but He promises to be with us every step of the way.

When we hand over our problems every day, it instills hope within us. In the psalm, we see that God raises us up; He restores us and protects us. What great hope that gives! If we cry out to the Lord for help, He will help us, according to His plan and His timing for our lives.

In 2011, my husband and I decided we were ready to have a baby. We had always dreamed of being parents and building a family together. We thought it would happen quickly because we loved each other very much and we were ready. Well, God was not ready to give us a baby. We tried to get pregnant for two years and were getting discouraged. I decided to visit my doctor and get some help. I was prescribed a fertility drug, and within two months I was pregnant!

I wanted to celebrate, tell my entire family, buy a crib, and paint the nursery. However, only two weeks later, I had a miscarriage. I was devastated. Here I was, with my first pregnancy after trying for over two years, and it ended with such grief! I began to question why God allowed this to happen. He knew how much we were trying and how much we wanted a baby. Where was God in this?

God never left me. He was with me from the conception of our baby until the death of our baby. Psalm 30:4-6 says, "Weeping may last through the night, but joy comes with the morning." This verse gave me hope in the midst of my pain. Through the loss, I began to read my Bible and pray more. I suddenly stopped fretting so much about getting pregnant and feeling upset that it was not easy for us to conceive. I just had this peace about the whole situation.

A few months later, I was blessed with another pregnancy. I could not have been more thrilled. This pregnancy brought us our precious son, Brody. A couple of years later, we were excited to bring home his little brother, Blake.

How could I still be upset with God over how things did not go the way I had planned? Through this journey, God has taught me to put my hope in Him. He taught me that it's ok to give up control and let His hand intercede. God instilled such hope and peace within me, and I am so thankful that He did!

So I have said all of that to say this: Hand. Over. Problems. Every day (HOPE). We will have problems. Jesus told us that in scripture. He did not design our lives to be rainbows and butterflies all the time. I truly believe that God allows us to journey through difficult times to draw us closer to Him, for He is always there for us and will never leave us, even in our darkest times.

I challenge you to thank God for your trials. Thank Him for helping you through them and for guiding you every step of the way. God is good all the time. All we have to do is allow Him to turn our mourning into joyful dancing, and clothe us with His joy (Psalm 30:11-13).

Reflecting on the reading:

1. *Have you given God total control over your life?*

2. *How can you thank God for the trials in your life?*

3. *This week, how can you be clothed in joy?*

Weekly readings: Acts 5:27-32, 40b-41; Psalm 30:2, 4-6, 11-13; Revelation 5:11-14; John 21:1-19

Carrying the White Coat Cross

-DR. ANNE VALERI WHITE

After this I had a vision of a great multitude, which no one could count, from every nation, race, people, and tongue. They stood before the throne and before the Lamb, wearing white robes and holding palm branches in their hands.

REVELATION 7:9

I found myself face to face with Our Lady holding her Son's body as anguish crumpled her beautiful countenance. This wasn't an apparition or a dream. Rather, it was a pietà near the altar of the Sorrowful Mother Shrine, where numerous miraculous healings have occurred. In the Blessed Mother's hand somebody had placed a folded note with a desperate plea. I touched her hand, careful not to disturb the petition, and humbly requested my own healing.

I took in my surroundings, fascinated by the many crutches that lined the altar. No doubt these were left by the faithful who experienced true miracles. "Please heal my heart," I whispered, fighting back a swell of tears.

The fact that I can cry at all is evidence of a healing that has already taken place. At one point in my career, the emotional exhaustion I experienced was so deep that I physically could not cry. I am currently fighting another fierce battle with burnout, after emerging from its shadows two short years ago. In the years since my initial healing, many drastic changes occurred at work at a time when I had become too self-reliant, too confident, and too proud. I found myself in a familiar tailspin.

All I ever wanted to be was a good doctor, but it wasn't enough for me to accomplish my life's goal. By God's design, I thirst for more. My heart longs for the miracles I haven't seen in medicine. I want to be a true healer; but that is His work, not mine. Instead of helping the lame to walk and the blind to see, my world is one of computers, quality metrics, and an ever-losing battle to do more in less time. I struggle to make peace with this desolation and use it for His unrevealed purpose.

In a nation where we lose 400 physicians per year to suicide, despair among medical professionals is common and hope is sparse. Dismayed, I have witnessed the wellbeing of my mentors and friends completely unravel. My own spirit is deeply wounded from a decade of burnout. I want to walk away from medicine, but I know that this is not His will.

Instead, I am surviving this time of great distress with the hope that God will wipe away every tear from my eyes. I have faith that He destined me for more than this suffering, which, in His eyes is so small and brief.

For me, there are no crutches to lay down at the altar. There is only a small ember of hope that will not extinguish. It is sufficient. Eventually, the Spirit will call me to shake the dust from my feet, rejoicing in the places where He leads. I wait for this new calling while stoking the embers of hope with works of mercy. Meanwhile I take up the cross of my white coat every day, asking for the intercession of our Sorrowful Mother and the great multitude who have washed their robes and made them white in the blood of the Lamb.

Ultimately, I'll trade my white coat for a similar robe… I hope.

Reflecting on the reading:

1. *In what aspect of your life have you experienced a healing?*

2. *Did it come in the form you had expected?*

3. *Who in the great multitude do you rely on for intercession?*

Weekly readings: Acts 13:14, 43-52; Psalm 100:1-3, 5; Revelation 7:9, 14b-17; John 10:27-30

Goodnight

-RUTH CLIFFORD

Then I saw a new heaven and a new earth. The former heaven and the former earth had passed away, and the sea was no more.

REVELATION 21:1

I met my husband 10 years ago and it wasn't long after I met him that I started to meet his family. I remember the first time I went to breakfast at his mom's house. She pulled out her finest china to impress me (and perhaps secretly hoping that I might be awed by this beautiful presentation and stick around a little longer). The greatest highlight of that breakfast was not the food or the beautiful crystal. The greatest highlight of that morning was meeting Grandmother Dear.

At that time, Grandmother Dear was eighty-six years old. She was the sweetest, cutest thing in the world. She just had a way about her that made the world a better place. There was a calm in her and a peace like no other. It was very evident that she loved her family more than anything in the world. She only had an eighth grade education so she mispronounced words all the time, which made her even more endearing. She grew up in Arkansas on the cotton fields and she would tell wonderful stories of the chickens she and her family had and memories of growing up with her mischievous siblings.

It wasn't too long after my husband and I began dating that he decided to move back home with his mom and Grandmother Dear, to help them out, which provided even more opportunity for me to spend time with Grandmother Dear. We would sit in the living room and talk. She would tell me that the name "Dear" came from her son wanting to call her "Mother Dear." He couldn't pronounce the "mother" as a child so it became "Ma'Dear," which eventually was shortened to just "Dear."

She would tell me about her children and how hard it was raising them, being a stay-at-home mom, while her husband (whom she lovingly referred to as "Daddy") would go to work as a chef. And she never failed to share with me about her love for God and how He had been her sustainer through all these years. She sadly talked about the days when she would take the kids to church every Sunday while Daddy stayed at home because he didn't really believe. But then her face would light up as she spoke about the day he went to church with her and the kids and gave his life to Christ.

Over the years, I grew even closer to Grandmother Dear. We would brainstorm Christmas ideas together because she didn't have much money but she wanted to give everyone a little something. I introduced her to Pinterest and inexpensive creative ideas. One of our favorite Christmas gifts that we gave her grandchildren was a personalized letter from her to each of them. It was my favorite gift because it gave me an opportunity to sit and listen to her speak about her love for each of her grandchildren.

Her health began to deteriorate soon after that Christmas. At ninety-four, Grandmother Dear took her last breath.

During her dimmer hours of this life, she saw something awesome on the other side. She whispered the words "it is beautiful." I don't know what she saw. Perhaps she saw the golden street, the pearl gates, or the crystal seas. Perhaps she saw the beautiful face of our Savior.

Her last word in this life was "goodnight."

With her simple goodnight, she was reminding us that there will be a new earth, a new heaven, a new order of things, and that leaving us here on earth was not a goodbye but just a goodnight... until we see one another again.

And so this is where my hope lies. In this life, there will be pain, sorrow, tears, and death. But oh the joy to know that there is something on the other side of this! And it is beautiful!

Goodnight.

Reflecting on the reading:

1. *What is your favorite memory of your grandparents? What do you cherish from them?*

2. *Have you felt the pain of losing a loved one? How did you find hope?*

3. *When faced with loss and pain, how can you focus on the "beautiful" joy waiting on the other side?*

Weekly readings: Acts 14:21-27; Psalm 145:8-13; Revelation 21:1-5a; John 13:31-33a, 34-35

No More Butterfly Kisses

-VICKI PRZYBYLSKI

Peace I leave with you; my peace I give to you. Not as the world gives do I give it to you. Do not let your hearts be troubled or afraid.

JOHN 14:27

I long for the days when a hug, a Band-Aid or a sticker could solve the problems of the world for my children. Telling them that Daddy and I love them and that Jesus was watching over them was enough to give them reassurance until the next crisis hit. Then, they grew up. My children are now twenty-four, twenty-two and fourteen years old, respectively. They still welcome my hugs, and know we love them, but solving their problems now takes on a whole new meaning. Many times, their problems are out of my control, and that does not sit well with me at all.

As a police officer, I respond to crisis situations every day, assess them quickly and take control and fix them (at least temporarily). But as a mom, it is sometimes more complicated than that, and I am left feeling out of control and having to turn to Jesus for His help. The Lord always reminds me of His peace, and that I need not let my heart be troubled or afraid (John 14:27). Sometimes that is easier said than done.

My daughter was married to the love of her life. They had been together for years and we knew and loved him. He spent a lot of time with us as a family and we came to love him like he was one of our own. A year after they were married, they moved from their apartment into his mom's house to help her with the bills. Soon after the move, he became very controlling, verbally abusive and eventually threatened physical harm. My daughter hid this well, and we had no idea what she had been dealing with day to day. She eventually left him, letting go of the nightmare that had started as a fairytale.

I was so shocked and brokenhearted; I didn't know how to react. I began to pray for my daughter, for her faith and for a new beginning. I prayed that the Lord's plan in all this would be revealed. She was heartbroken, destroyed and embarrassed. I was confused and angry. Confused because we had prayed so hard for this marriage to be successful, and angry because I did not see the signs. How could I deal with situations like this, fifty-plus hours a week, and not see it happening in my own family?

As a mom, the hardest part was that I was not able to protect her from this. How do you Band-Aid the heart? I asked the Lord, "Why didn't you let me protect her?" That is when I heard Him say to my heart, "I have always been there with her." So I decided to choose hope. I decided to set aside the despair, anger and confusion and climb into my Abba's lap and let Him hug me and tell me it would be ok because He loves me. I decided to let His plan for my daughter's life run its course and see what the Lord had in store for her.

My daughter was eventually offered a promotion at her job. She would have to move two hours away, but she would be doing something she loved for twice the pay. Most importantly, she would be given a fresh start and a renewed sense of purpose for her life.

The days of butterfly kisses and quick fixes may be gone. It may take more than a hug, a Band-Aid or a sticker to solve the problems of the world for my children. But they do know that their father and I love them and are here for them, and most of all, they know that the love and presence of the Lord is everlasting.

Reflecting on the reading:

1. Have you ever felt like your life was out of control?

2. This week, read John 14:23-29 and reflect on the peace that can only come from God.

3. How can you allow the Lord to bring you peace through life's chaotic moments?

Weekly readings: Acts 15:1-2, 22-29; Psalm 67:2-3, 5-6, 8;
Revelation 21:10-14, 22-23; John 14:23-29

Following the Apostles

-ELENA LAVICTOIRE

When he had said this, as they were looking on, he was lifted up, and a cloud took him from their sight. While they were looking intently at the sky as he was going…

ACTS 1:9-10a

Reading this part of the Book of Acts always puts a lump in my throat and a tear in my eye. I feel such sadness for these poor disciples as they watch their Friend, Teacher, and Savior disappear from their midst never to be seen again, at least not in the way they were used to seeing Him.

Everyone experiences that feeling of loss at some point. I know that feeling too well, the grief of losing a loved one - grandparents, parents, beloved friends, relatives. I also know that the older I get, the more loss I will experience. I often joke with my husband that one of us isn't getting out of this marriage alive! Sooner or later one of us will have to live through the unspeakable loss of losing the other. Until then, as we grow old together, we will experience other losses.

Let's face it. I am no longer the pretty twenty-year-old bride I once was. I have given birth to children and I have the stretch marks to prove it. The years of anxiety and worry have left me with frosted silvery tresses, too numerous to pluck out any more. And like it or not, I now have a knee that reminds me once in a while that I can't just go out and hike without stretching and wearing appropriate shoes anymore. In many ways it feels like growing older is a loss of its own, a loss of times gone by, experiences I can't relive.

The disciples must have been feeling the same way. Their days of walking and talking with Jesus, listening to His parables and witnessing His miracles were over for them as well.

Yet this is just a very small part of this Book of Acts. St. Luke, the good doctor to the people, doesn't allow the reader to dwell on the loss of Jesus. He goes on to write, "They were looking intently up into the sky as he was going, when suddenly two men dressed in white stood beside them. 'Men of Galilee,' they said, 'why do you stand here looking into the sky? This same Jesus, who has been taken from you into heaven, will come back in the same way you have seen him go into heaven'" (Acts 1:10-11).

Jesus has gone to heaven, but we can take hope in the knowledge that He will return. So why do we waste time looking into the sky? Why do we waste time feeling sad? Indeed, in the very next chapter, the apostles return to Jerusalem and get on with the work of God, for their journey was just beginning.

I am sure they were still a little sad, but the angels God sent to encourage them inspired them to have hope and to carry on.

It's hard to accept loss. Sometimes it's appropriate to fight it. I lost weight and strengthened my weak knee so that I could do the things I love to do. Hopefully I will get more pain free years out of it, providing I continue to strengthen and stretch it while maintaining a lower body weight.

Other losses are harder to accept. My mother's death was particularly difficult to accept. I still miss her voice and her presence in my life every day. But just as the angels promised the apostles they would see Jesus again, I have hope of seeing my mom again in heaven for I know she believed in her salvation through Jesus Christ. Through her example and teaching, she passed that faith on to me. That hope is what enables me to get on with my life after her passing, just as the apostles got on with theirs after the ascension.

With hope and joy, Christians can follow the example of the apostles as told to us by St. Luke, because we know that someday He will come back in the same way from heaven. Whether I am working out my salvation here, or in the next life, I hope to be part of that!

Reflecting on the reading:

1. What feelings did the disciples have as they watched Jesus as He was taken up into the heavens?

2. What loss have you experienced that has been difficult to overcome?

3. How can you find peace and hope in the love of Christ and His return as you journey through your loss?

Weekly readings: Acts 1:1-11; Psalm 47:2-3, 6-9; Ephesians 1:17-23 or Hebrews 9:24-28; 10:19-23; Luke 24:46-53

Veni Sancte Spiritus

-BETTY SCHNITZLER

When the time for Pentecost was fulfilled, they were all in one place together.
And suddenly there came from the sky a noise like a strong driving wind,
and it filled the entire house in which they were.

ACTS 2:1-2

Veni Sancte Spiritus. Three simple words, but when our pastor begins to chant these words at the beginning of his homily, amazing things happen.

Our story begins in May of 2017, a week after my mom passed away. My family was mourning the loss of a beautiful Catholic soul and a spiritual leader for our family. My daughter, Monica, has had medical issues since she was a small child, including seizures, which have occurred randomly throughout her life. Her neurologist made a decision to admit Monica to the hospital for a week of intense study, which would include forcing a seizure in order to determine what was causing these disruptions in Monica's brain. Her hospital stay was scheduled for the Monday after Pentecost. Needless to say, Monica was very nervous about the hospitalization.

On Pentecost Sunday, my husband, Monica, and I were in our usual places at the 11:00 Mass. Monica was on my left and Greg was on my right. When Father Bline began to chant *"Veni Sancte Spiritus,"* the entire congregation joined in. As he began his homily, Father Bline asked us all an important question: "Do you know what you have just done? You have invited the Holy Spirit to come to you."

From the time we had entered the church that day, Monica's nervousness had caused a headache that was spreading down the back of her neck. As Father Bline was preaching his homily, Monica heard a gentle voice calmly whisper her name. She looked around, thinking that someone in a nearby pew was speaking to her. No one was speaking at that time, as we were all listening to the homily. Once more, she heard someone whisper her name, "Monica." At the same time that she heard the voice speak her name, she felt a breeze blowing on her face, as if the Holy Spirit was trying to get her attention. Suddenly, the same calm voice spoke to her saying, "Do not be afraid! Everything will be ok. Just stay calm, have faith and trust in Me."

As the Holy Spirit spoke to Monica, she felt the presence of her grandma sitting next to her. Her headache went away completely and was replaced with a feeling of peace and calm that can only come from God. Monica and I both had felt the presence of her grandma (my mom) sitting in the pew between us. She had been such a blessing to us in life and was now blessing us from her eternal home.

As we approached Father Bline for communion, he spoke to Monica when he presented the Eucharist to her. His words were, "Everything will be OK." He also spoke to me, saying, "I am praying for you right now," and to my husband, saying, "Trust." The Holy Spirit and Father Bline both shared a beautiful, powerful message of hope to Monica on that special Sunday.

Monica entered the hospital with a wonderful sense of calm and peace like I had never seen in the past. She continued to feel the presence of her grandma and the calming touch of the Holy Spirit as she was admitted to the hospital and spent a full week in testing. *Veni Sancte Spiritus.* Three simple words and the touch of the Holy Spirit. What an amazing sense of peace He can bring.

Reflecting on the reading:

1. *Was there ever a time when you felt the Lord speaking directly to you?*

2. *Were you able to answer Him with hope and peace?*

3. *This week, how can you be the voice of the Lord and bring peace to anyone you encounter?*

Weekly readings: Acts 2:1-11; Psalm 104:1, 24, 29-31, 34; 1 Corinthians 12:3b-7, 12-13 or Romans 8:8-17; John 20:19-23 or John 14:15-16, 23b-26

NOT Disappointed!

-PASTOR LINDA ISAIAH

Not only that, but we even boast of our afflictions, knowing that affliction produces
endurance, and endurance, proven character, and proven character, hope...
ROMANS 5:3-4

As I sit in front of my computer screen with tears running down my face, I'm thinking about this particular season of my life. Who would have thought that last year at this time my husband would be dead, and after thirty-six years of marriage I would be moving out of our home? What happened to our happily ever after?

There are days when I'm exhausted from crying, sleepless nights, people asking me, "How are you doing?" I am exhausted from too many phone calls concerning my husband, making decisions, putting gas in the car. I can feel the nagging shadow of hopelessness cascading over me like a dark cloud, and I am left wondering if I will ever get over Erroll's passing.

The pain was taking my breath away. On top of moving, I had a sixteen-year-old son who was grieving the loss of his father and looking to me for all of his emotional needs. I felt as if I were drowning, without energy to fight for my survival. Even still, I relive the days of his passing over and over again in my mind.

I had dropped Erroll off at the hospital for a minor medical procedure that he had endured on many occasions. All other times I'd stayed with him through his procedure, but on this day, he told me to go home and get some rest. It was on December 4, 2017, that he developed a blood clot in his right arm that broke off and traveled down his hand.

I received a call from the hospital to come back immediately.

I cried a little and went to the hospital. I was grateful the hospital was only five minutes from my house. I arrived, signed in and had a seat. I decided to go to the gift shop for chocolate. While in the gift shop I heard a code blue over the speakers. I thought in my mind, "Is that Erroll?" My faith wouldn't let me go there. (By the way, I chose cheese popcorn over chocolate.) While waiting, a doctor came to tell me that Erroll had stopped breathing and had gone into cardiac arrest. He was no longer stable.

I was in shock and crying uncontrollably. As a pastor, and speaker, I was supposed to be the hope dispenser - but all of my hope was being challenged. In Romans 5:3-4, we read: "Not only that, but we even boast of our afflictions, knowing that affliction produces endurance, and endurance, proven character, and proven character, hope." But I could not see that hope very clearly.

As I sat in the hospital, everything felt like it was happening in slow motion. Friends and family came. Prayer warriors prayed. Erroll was placed in ICU, heavily sedated. He kept trying to talk and write. I kept his writings. I had the difficult task of calling our son, one of the hardest calls I have had to make.

When you make the decision to face your suffering with the Lord, you can get through anything. I dug deep in my spiritual reserve and pushed through my anguish, not knowing what was going to be the outcome. I knew Erroll was very sick. I also knew he was in God's hands and all I could do was pray. I left the hospital, went home and slept very well. I was resting in God's hope for me and my family.

Erroll came out of this ordeal talking and laughing. I was so grateful to God. He stayed in the hospital for ten days and came home with an oxygen tank. It was unbearable at times. He wouldn't sleep for fear of dying. Tears. Painful.

My Honey died 17 days later.

It's been eight months and I'm still in shock.

My sufferings have brought about perseverance and character and have left me with hope that can only come from Jesus. I made a choice in that waiting room to choose hope. My life has changed forever, but my Jesus will never change, He will never let me down.

Life will disappoint us. But God never will!

Reflecting on the reading:

1. *Can you remember a time in your life when you felt hopeless? Explain.*

2. *How do you handle disappointment with God?*

3. *Do you have your hope back?*

Weekly readings: Proverbs 8:22-31; Psalm 8:4-9; Romans 5:1-5; John 16:12-15

Mission: Possible

-FR. NATHAN CROMLY

Then taking the five loaves and the two fish, and looking up to heaven, he said the blessing over them, broke them, and gave them to the disciples to set before the crowd. They all ate and were satisfied.

LUKE 9:16-17a

Sometimes, God really surprises me. When He asks us to do things that are within our power, we can all agree that it is reasonable to serve Him by our obedience. But what do we say when He asks us to do the impossible? Do we follow when He bids us walk on water?

Our scriptural passage today contains an impossible mission. The apostles face a significant human problem: massive crowds of hungry people. They contrive a human solution, suggesting that the people be sent off on their own to find food. But Christ challenges them to adopt a more personal and yet seemingly impossible approach: "Give them something yourselves to eat."

The mission they are challenged by Christ to live out is, from a human perspective, impossible. The apostles simply cannot provide an impromptu meal for thousands upon thousands of people! And, don't we feel the same way so many times as we follow Him? Why does He do this to us?

The answer is as beautiful as it is simple: The only way for you to do the impossible is to rely upon Someone who can. The only way forward is to cross the threshold of hope in God.

"With God, nothing will be impossible" (Luke 1:37). Christ manifests this in the Gospel by using a few loaves of bread to feed thousands, the food gratuitously overflowing into baskets of leftovers. Why would we doubt that He wants to do the same with us? Why would He be any less faithful to our daring something for Him? Couldn't His bounty overflow in our world as well?

I am always amazed at just how important hope in God is – not just to us, but to God! So many times in the Gospel, Jesus challenges His apostles to broaden their perspectives and to stretch themselves. The lives of the Saints are filled with this same stretching. And our world is better for it!

For us, when we hear God's call and dare the impossible in response, we discover hope.

Hope means relying on God to accomplish what He has asked you to do, regardless of whether it feels possible. When you give your day to Him, He can use you to multiply the laughter in someone's life, the love someone knows or the capacity someone has to receive the Word of God. Trusting in the power of God creates more than enough; it overflows into leftovers.

This theme of God responding gratuitously to hope is beautifully present in what happened for a little community, the Sisters of Loretto, in Santa Fe, New Mexico in the late nineteenth century. When the Sisters found themselves with a chapel that was too small for a staircase but had no access to the choir loft, they faced an impossible mission. Yet they placed their trust in God, beginning a novena to St. Joseph, patron of carpenters. At the end of the novena, a man with a hammer showed up, built a magnificent staircase, complete with two 360-degree turns, and vanished without waiting to be paid.

The Sisters invited grace to work in their situation and guide their human process, and, in an astonishing way, God responded to their hope and transformed their situation. As the story of the Sisters of Loretto shows, it's not a question of the size of your mission, but of the size of the courage, trust and hope with which you undertake it.

Hope is possible because there is something beyond your material existence; there is a God who came down from Heaven to seek your personal love. God is there for you to rely on in the impossible hurts and perplexities of heartbreak, illness and death. He is also there for you to rely on in the problems of missing staircases and hungry stomachs. God wants you to trust Him even as you make your plans for today.

Nothing is impossible for God, and nothing is impossible for the one who believes in God. As Mother Angelica liked to say, "To get the miraculous, you have to attempt the ridiculous!" And though not everything works out according to earthly measures, love and confidence have triumphed where hope was dared. And, maybe, to God, this is what matters the most!

Reflecting on the reading:

1. *Have you ever faced an impossible situation, by earthly standards?*

2. *How can you ask God for the impossible and have hope in the outcome?*

3. *Reflect on Mother Angelica's words: "To get the miraculous, you have to attempt the ridiculous!"*

Weekly readings: Genesis 14:18-20; Psalm 110:1-4; 1 Corinthians 11:23-26; Luke 9:11b-17

June 30, 2019 (13th Sunday in Ordinary Time)

Confidence in God

-PASTOR JOHN MULPAS

For you will not abandon my soul to Sheol, nor let your devout one see the pit.
You will show me the path to life, abounding joy in your presence, the delights at your
right hand forever.

PSALM 16:10-11

As a father of three, I keep fairly busy with my kids' activities. I really enjoy being there for their games and concerts. This year, my son is running cross country for the first time. It has been a new experience for our entire family. It's fun to watch him run and cheer him on. "Go! You can do it!" I'm pretty sure my presence is an encouragement to my son and makes him feel valued, even though he doesn't like to be seen as much with Dad anymore (he turned thirteen this year).

Much more significant than my presence with my son is God's presence with us. Our heavenly Father is always with us. It's one of the greatest promises in Scripture. David puts it this way in Psalm 16:8: "I keep the Lord always before me; with him at my right hand, I shall never be shaken." What an encouragement! What hope!

We're not sure of the specific setting or circumstances that prompted David to write these words, but I imagine his showdown with Goliath was on his mind. You know the story. David was a teenager, probably around sixteen years old. Goliath was a grown man and over nine feet tall. David had his shepherd's staff, five stones and a sling. Goliath had all the best weaponry and armor, all made of bronze. It was clear who was going to win this fight. Goliath, of course! But no, in the end, it was David who won. How? Because God was with him, right beside him. As David proclaimed, "The battle is the Lord's."

Through this experience and others, David's confidence was in God's presence. This is further illustrated throughout Psalm 16: "Keep me safe, O God; in you I take refuge" (v.1). "I keep the Lord always before me; with him at my right hand, I shall never be shaken" (v.8). "For you will not abandon my soul to Sheol, nor let your devout one see the pit" (v.10).

The same can be true for me and for you. We can have confidence in God's presence too, and that is where our hope lies. If you're doubting God's presence today, remember past victories, times in your life when God saw you through a difficult time, brought you out of darkness. David remembered his victory over Goliath and others and that memory gave him confidence in God's presence.

Count your blessings, giving thanks for every good thing in your life, as every good thing comes from God. David said, "You are my Master! Every good thing I have comes from you" (Psalm 16:2 NLT). All of the good things He has given you point to His presence in your life, and you can find confidence and hope in that.

It's no accident the final verses of Psalm 16 are quoted twice in the New Testament (Acts 2:25-28; 13:35). They foretell the death and resurrection of Jesus, and ultimately, our resurrection at His second coming. How awesome is that? God is always with us, even in death! "For you will not leave my soul among the dead… You will show me the way of life, granting me the joy of your presence and the pleasures of living with you forever" (Psalm 16:10-11 NLT).

Like David, God's presence gives us confidence in life and in death. We can face our "Goliaths" because He is always there, right beside us. So, do not be shaken. There is hope!

Dear Father, I come to You for refuge, counsel and hope. Thank You for always being with me. Even though I don't always feel You, I know You are there. Your promises are so good! Give me confidence to face whatever comes my way. I need you. In Jesus' name, amen.

Reflecting on the reading:

1. *What challenges are you facing this week? Do they seem insurmountable?*

2. *How can you trust in God's presence, like David, and seek His voice daily?*

3. *How can your prayer life reflect your confidence in God's presence in your life?*

Weekly readings: 1 Kings 19:16b, 19-21; Psalm 16:1-2, 5, 7-11; Galatians 5:1, 13-18; Luke 9:51-62

Unseen Restoration

-PAM LILE

Shall I bring a mother to the point of birth, and yet not let her child be born? says the Lord.
Or shall I who bring to birth yet close her womb? says your God.

ISAIAH 66:9

It was around three years ago when I was led into a conversation with God. Though not an audible voice, it had a profound beginning followed by a still small voice whispering to my heart. Through this conversation, my desire to know God, and to understand where He was leading me, was insatiable. I delighted in His little love notes that were sent to me each morning through Lectio Divina. My soul rejoiced in the little forget-me-nots all around me. It was the first time I could "hear" His voice in the movements of my soul.

Prayer was now lived throughout the day as a conversation that happened from the moment I woke in the morning until I drifted off to sleep at day's end. He would often call me to spend time with Him in adoration, finally leading me to daily Mass each morning. Little did I know the greatest trial of my life was about to begin, and my good God was preparing my heart to trust Him.

The timing was perfectly orchestrated the day my eight-year-old son screamed of a headache and fell unconscious in a matter of minutes. We had just arrived home from vacation a couple of days prior. My husband, Dave, had arrived home from work not ten minutes before, enabling us to respond immediately. As it turned out, Sam had a malformation of vessels that burst, causing a large bleed which stroked out half of his brain. It was the darkest of nights as his life hung in the balance.

I was suffocating. And yet a small thought pierced the darkness, offering a tiny glimmer of light. There are a million reasons why this should have happened another way, at another time - a time when we would not have been able to respond as quickly as we did. But it didn't happen that way. It happened at the perfect moment. This reflection on Divine Providence was enough to sustain me - and I clung to it. Jesus was reaching into my darkness and asking me to take His hand. He had prepared me well to turn towards Him during the past three years and that is what I did.

I talked to Jesus, even though I didn't have much to say at first. I just cried out to Him. But I offered Him what I had. I asked Him to take the groanings of my heart and turn them into a prayer because I was empty. Sam spent seventy-three days in the hospital and eventually breathed on his own, opened his eyes, and began to speak again. Eventually I found my words again too.

Often my words were full of praise, always they were sad as despair would slip in and weave a lonely web when my guard was down; but all the while I talked to God, and He always continued to speak very sweetly to me. He continued to offer me beautifully wrapped gifts in the whisper of His voice. The only thing He asked of me was that I continue to seek Him. In my joy, in my confusion, and in my profound sadness, all He asked of me was to lean on Him.

Our journey is not complete. The struggles remain as we suffer through Sam's limitations. Everything is a challenge for him. His left side remains dormant as he labors incredibly hard just to get through a day. But through God's Word, His love notes, we have the assurance that He is not finished with Sam yet, nor with me.

God does not "close up the womb" at the moment of delivery, rather He sees His work through to completion. God wants us to rejoice, to be satisfied, to delight in the abundance of His blessing. He wants peace and comfort to be restored to our troubled hearts just as a child rests in the arms of his mother. He has promised us that we won't merely survive, but that we will flourish.

From our current vantage point, we cling to the assurance that "the hand of the Lord will be made known to His servants." We choose to hope in Sam's future because God's Word continues to speak healing and restoration to our hearts. As we look forward to the restoration that remains unseen, we rejoice in the abundance that awaits us.

Reflecting on the reading:

1. Have you ever heard the still small voice of God whisper to you?

2. How do you rest in the hope of Jesus even though your journey is not complete and your struggles remain?

3. How can you pray this week for the restoration that remains unseen, and rejoice in the abundance that awaits you?

Weekly readings: Isaiah 66:10-14c; Psalm 66:1-7, 16, 20; Galatians 6:14-18; Luke 10:1-12, 17-20

In the Midst of Life

-MARCIA LICHI

For in him were created all things in heaven and on earth, the visible and the invisible,
whether thrones or dominions or principalities or powers;
all things were created through him and for him.

COLOSSIANS 1:16

In this year of our Lord, 2019, choosing hope is not always easy to do. When we listen to the news and read about current events, we are assailed by a feeling of hopelessness and cynicism at the brokenness that surrounds us. Evil seems to triumph far too often and sin and suffering abound. Even our physical world seems to groan as it endures both natural and man-made disasters that are increasing in frequency and ferocity. We often find it easier to be fearful rather than hopeful.

This time we live in and the condition of the world around us are exactly the reasons why it is absolutely essential to keep our eyes on Jesus. It is only in Him that we can choose hope because He is our hope! When we meditate on who Jesus is (Colossians 1:15-20) we see profound reasons to choose hope in knowing what He has done for us. Jesus is Supreme over all!

To begin with, you may be fearful and unable to trust God because you cannot see Him. Perhaps the father figure in your life was not a loving, safe person for you. This was my experience and thus I have had difficulty throughout my life trusting God the Father. How reassuring verses 15 and 19 are to us! "Christ is the visible image of the invisible God… For God in all his fullness was pleased to live in Christ." We only need to look at Jesus and how He lived his life to see the Father and know His heart. Jesus lived in constant fellowship with God the Father. He was very clear and transparent about the love relationship that flowed between them. When you are fearful because you can't see God, look at Jesus and get to know Him!

Next, when fear besets you as you consider the state of our physical world, choose hope because Jesus is "supreme over all creation. Everything was created through him and for him. He existed before anything else and he *holds all creation together"* (Colossians 1:16-17). Notice the use of the present tense in the verb "holds." We don't need to be fearful about what is happening to our world because Jesus is holding it all together, right now, in the present.

What about when we face death? Surely this is something most people are fearful of. Because Jesus rose from the dead after His sacrificial death on the cross, He provides eternal life for those who trust in Him. Verse 20 is the essence of the gospel: "He made peace with everything on heaven and on earth by means of Christ's blood on the cross."

I have a friend who is facing imminent death because of cancer. Unless the Lord intervenes, she will pass from this life very soon. However, she absolutely glories in the sure knowledge of her life being hidden with Christ and the minute she leaves this world she will be present with Him for all eternity. Now that is *hope!*

One of my favorite hymns of all time is "My Hope is Built on Nothing Less" (Edward Mote, 1797-1874). The first stanza recites the foundation for our hope: "My hope is built on nothing less than Jesus' blood and righteousness. I dare not trust the sweetest frame but wholly lean on Jesus' name." And again in the 3rd stanza, "His oath, His covenant, His blood support me in the whelming flood; when every earthly prop gives way He then is all my Hope and Stay. On Christ the Solid Rock I stand, all other ground is sinking sand, all other ground is sinking sand."

In this year of our Lord, 2019, choosing hope is the only option for a Christian. Our hope is in Jesus, and that never changes, no matter how the world groans.

Reflecting on the reading:

1. Do you watch the news regularly and are you sad at the state of the world today?

2. Are there circumstances from your past that make it difficult to trust your Father in heaven?

3. How can you plant your hope firmly on the solid rock of Jesus Christ?

Weekly readings: Deuteronomy 30:10-14; Psalm 69:14, 17, 30-31, 33-34, 36-37; Colossians 1:15-20; Luke 10:25-37

Impossible Dreams

-MARK PICCOLINO

One of them said, "I will return to you about this time next year, and Sarah will then have a son." Sarah was listening at the entrance of the tent, just behind him.

GENESIS 18:10

In our suburban Pittsburgh backyard, you can see the area wildlife--from the groundhogs who burrow under our shed every year to a number of deer, rabbits, stray cats, squirrels, various families of wild turkeys and, of course, a variety of birds. We even had a skunk wander through our yard a couple of years ago. This year we have seen an even greater variety of birds. We had a nest of sparrows in a bush next to our driveway; our neighbors had an oriole nest and a robin's nest. Our daughter had a wren build a nest in the hanging basket on her porch, and this year we actually had a hummingbird nest in the tree in our front yard.

With the plethora of bird sightings this year it reminded me of a time a few years back when I was gazing out our kitchen window and noticed a number of sparrows fluttering around the cyclone fence that divides our driveway from our neighbor's yard.

The sparrows would perch in the little squares in the fence then fly and land on the driveway. Then they would turn around and fly back and do it again. After a while, I figured out that they were flying through the tall grass growing alongside the driveway to shake free the grass seeds so they could eat them. I was amazed that these tiny birds would know how to do that.

Watching for a while, I was reminded of the Bible verse in Luke: "Consider the ravens: they do not sow or reap, they have no storeroom or barn; yet God feeds them. And how much more valuable you are than birds!" (Luke 12:24).

What hope we have is in the assurance that God loves us and we are valuable to Him.

Abraham and Sarah saw that hope and value first hand when the Lord told Abraham that even though Sarah was older, she would conceive a child. Exciting news? Maybe. Prophecy? Definitely. Abraham and Sarah tried for years to have a child. Now that they were old and past childbearing years they got news that they were to have a child. Hope must have been one of the emotions they were experiencing, but so was concern. Would she be able to carry full term? Would she be able to endure childbirth at her age? I'm sure Abraham had his own doubts about raising a child at his age and still leading his people.

I'm not sure where you are in your life, but as for my wife and me, I'm sure we would be a little overwhelmed at the thought of having a child at our age and we are definitely not near the ages of Abraham and Sarah.

Imagine Abraham and Sarah's hope born from God's own words that they would conceive and have a child at their ages. Being told by God that their heirs would outnumber the stars. How daunting a thought. How comforting a dream. Abraham and Sarah would finally have the child they desired, a son they named Isaac, which translated from the Hebrew means "he laughs."

Are you struggling with an impossible situation in your own life? Are you waiting for an answer to prayer? Looking to change careers? Buying a house or a new car? Looking for direction in your life? Wherever you are right now, you can find hope in the God who cares for the wildlife in your backyard, who feeds the sparrows seeds of grass.

The same God who took the impossible and made it possible for Abraham and Sarah can bring laughter into your life, too.

Reflecting on the reading:

1. *What are you struggling with today? What is stressing you out?*

2. *How can you turn your stress over to God?*

3. *How can your prayer life reflect your trust in God's plan for your life?*

Weekly readings: Genesis 18:1-10a; Psalm 15:2-5; Colossians 1:24-28; Luke 10:38-42

Ask God for the Extraordinary

-DR. DONALD A. LICHI

But he persisted: "Please, do not let my Lord be angry if I speak up this last time. What if ten are found there?" For the sake of the ten, he replied, I will not destroy it.

GENESIS 18:32

Have you ever asked God for something extraordinary? Or have you "negotiated" with God? Perhaps it was dealing with an illness. "Oh God, if You will only heal me then I will…" Maybe it was with a prodigal child. "Oh God, if You will only bring my child back to the Church I will…" Or maybe it was in the midst of a crisis. "Please, God, help me out of this crisis and I promise I will…"

You get the idea. Something really big, something extraordinary. Maybe God came through with what you asked. Did you follow through on your end of the bargain? Did you stop a negative behavior? Did you start a positive one?

Facing a difficult life or death situation, Abraham negotiated with God. Agents of God (some say a pre-incarnate presence of Christ) revealed that the evil and despicable cities of Sodom and Gomorrah were in danger of being destroyed. The people of these cities were beyond the pale of redemption and yet Abraham showed great mercy and love.

Abraham asked God for something truly extraordinary. He negotiated with God. The Bible says, "Abraham remained standing before the Lord." (Genesis 18: 22). Was he being bold (or just plain crazy) to stand up to God? The scripture says that their sin was so grievous that God wanted to see for Himself if things were as bad as they seemed (v 21). Abraham realized that perhaps some righteous people in the cities were in imminent danger of destruction. The angel-destroyers turned away and began their travel to Sodom and Gomorrah.

But Abraham stood his ground before the Lord. He appealed to God's mercy on behalf of the cities. "Seriously, God…if there are at least fifty righteous people there…will you really destroy them with everyone else?"

God said, "No." Abraham kept asking for the extraordinary. "What about forty-five?" Same answer. More negotiation with God. More concessions. The conversation continued until Abraham finally asked for one last extraordinary thing: "If there are only ten righteous people will you spare the cities?" God said yes - if there were even ten people, the cities would be spared.

Apparently, there were not even ten righteous people in those cities. You know the rest of the story.

Abraham really didn't get God to change His mind on anything. God knew there was no righteousness left in Sodom and Gomorrah. Amazingly, God did not criticize Abraham for asking for the extraordinary. In fact, Abraham was humble, honoring and trusting God for the extraordinary.

What a lesson for us! You may be going through the most difficult time in your life right now. Ask God for the extraordinary. In other scriptures, Jesus says, "Ask, seek, knock!" "You have not because you ask not!" "If you ask anything in my Name…it will be done for you!"

Are you willing to ask God for the extraordinary? Is anything too hard for God? I want to challenge you to seriously consider how Abraham asked the extraordinary of God. He acknowledged the holiness and righteousness of God. He never accused God of being unfair. In fact, he really discovered the heart of God - which was to spare the cities if only a handful of righteous could be found. This was God's plan all along.

When you ask God for the extraordinary, you get to know the heart of God. God is good. God is fair. God is love. More importantly, God loves you. He values you. He is willing to forgive you. He is conforming you to the image of Christ. He will never (ever!) leave you alone! So, go ahead, ask God for the extraordinary!

Reflecting on the reading:

1. *What extraordinary requests can you bring before the Lord?*

2. *How can you trust God for the answer to your prayer?*

3. *When God does not answer the way you would have liked, how can you seek His will?*

Weekly readings: Genesis 18:20-32; Psalm 138:1-3, 6-8; Colossians 2:12-14; Luke 11:1-13

Things Above

-AMY DODEZ

Think of what is above, not of what is on earth.
COLOSSIANS 3:2

We wondered if she was singing in heaven or humming to the heavenly songs as she laid there on the eve of her heaven day, moaning or crying with each breath and unable to be soothed or comforted. In our earthly thinking it seemed she was in pain, but was she? Or was she already moving into the heavenly realm?

As humans and Christians we struggle so often with keeping our "minds on things above, not on earthly things" (Colossians 3:2). If only we could focus all the time on heaven and God and all Jesus has done for us, life wouldn't be so difficult and burdensome.

But we are human and we will always battle to keep our minds focused on Christ. And thankfully, when the Holy Spirit gives me the power to keep my mind on things above, I have a hope, a hope that carries me, encourages me, and gives me peace.

This hope carried me through my daughter Karrie's cancer journey, which began in July of 2005, close to her third birthday. She was diagnosed with neuroblastoma, which is a cancer that develops from nerve cells. Karrie's cancer was in her adrenal gland and metastasized to her right knee and right wrist. We called it "the bad guy" in her belly.

Treatments began that same month. It was awful to watch her get sick after treatments. But it was wonderful to see her smile return once we got past the sick days. Hope encouraged me as I rode the roller coaster of ups and downs through each month that followed.

After seven months of chemotherapy, a stem cell transplant during a four-week hospital stay, two weeks of daily radiation, and then several months of drug therapy, Karrie was cancer free for four years. Hope gave me peace even when I struggled with the thought of the cancer returning like the statistics showed it would.

In March of 2010, the cancer did return in her right knee. After more chemotherapy and radiation, plus a week-long total body radiation treatment, the cancer took over her body and Karrie flew home to heaven with Jesus on August 30, 2011. She was only nine years old. Where did my hope go then?

After losing a child, it seems all hope is gone. However, on many days I have found that hope is really all I have to keep me going. My hope in Jesus helps me focus on things above. I really want to see my girl again and Jesus has given me a hope of that happening, because I have trusted in Him. Without Jesus, none of us has hope.

I often wonder, as many do, how people who don't have faith in Jesus get through the loss of someone they dearly love, especially the loss of a child. Can you imagine not knowing if you will ever see that loved one again? Or not knowing where your loved one is now? How could you possibly have hope?

Not only do I have hope because of the promises in God's Word, I know where Karrie is. She is with Jesus. She often paints rainbows with Jesus, the Master Creator. She sings and dances without any pain holding her down. She plays dress up and has tea parties with her friend Taylor. She is free and loved and whole. And the hope of one day seeing all this is what keeps me going.

So when the things of this earth start to crowd in and steal your hope, look to Jesus and meditate on God's promises in His Word. "Set your minds on things above, not on earthly things" (Colossians 3:2). It is a choice you have to make every day. I choose hope and to focus on things above, where my girl is hanging out with the King of Kings. That gives me peace.

Reflecting on the reading:

1. *Have you experienced extraordinary loss in this life?*

2. *Who has helped you journey through the pain and suffering?*

3. *How can you set your mind on things above, not earthly things?*

Weekly readings: Ecclesiastes 1:2; 2:21-23; Psalm 90:3-6, 12-14, 17; Colossians 3:1-5, 9-11; Luke 12:13-21

the Sacred Heart of Jesus
-EMILY JAMINET

Do not be afraid any longer, little flock, for your Father is pleased to give you the kingdom.
LUKE 12:32

Jesus provides us with a pathway to heaven through loving Him and developing a personal relationship with Him. In the Scriptures (Luke 12:32-48) we learn about how the Master returns home and discovers the state of the house. When I read this, I can't help but ponder the state of my own house. What would the Lord think if He walked in the door in the midst of family struggles, sibling bickering and fighting over petty matters? Or if the house is silent and everyone plugged in and on their devices?

The Master will arrive during an hour when the servant least expects Him, and He is willing to offer His blessings for those who are vigilant and faithful and will punish those who are not. What is the state of your home? Do you live in a way that welcomes Christ?

There are many times I walk in the door after leaving the older children in charge and find them utterly unready for my return. The to-do list has been untouched, and it is evident by the state of the house that they did not expect my return for a long time. The dishes are everywhere and the teenagers are chilling as the youngest ones are watching TV. As frustrating as that is, I am just as guilty of living an unready life when it comes to Christ's return.

So how can we live our lives as the faithful servants? How can we be prepared for the Master's return and know that, if we are prepared, we can inherit the Kingdom?

I have found that embedding myself in the heart of Christ has given me a lifeline of support and helps me live out my faith even when life is difficult. *The Sacred Heart Devotion* is a powerful devotion that has taught me to see Christ as one who is not only longing to be welcomed into my heart and home, but as a Friend who wants to help.

Five years ago, my family and I participated in a ceremony where we welcomed Christ to rule as King, Brother and Friend in our home through the Enthronement to the Sacred Heart. This Christian ceremony is grounded in the Twelve Promises of those who honor the Sacred Heart given to St. Margaret Mary Alacoque in the 1670's. He told her, "I will bless the homes in which the image of My Sacred Heart shall be exposed and honored."

When we are willing to allow Christ into our daily lives in the good times and bad, we give Christ new authority to rule in our homes, and in our families. This ceremony was the beginning of my family understanding how essential it is to welcome Christ into our lives, helping us to live in the world but not be of the world (John 17:14-15).

When we fail to welcome Christ into our lives or invite Him into our homes as King, Brother and Friend, He cannot help us. In so many homes, He knocks and waits at the door, wanting to come in and help, but He is never invited in. This ceremony is an opportunity to receive new graces and marks a new beginning in your life. Change can happen with the help of Christ.

In our home, we are learning to live out the Scripture "as for me and my house we shall serve the Lord" (Joshua 24:15b). When you seek the treasure of heaven and are not distracted by the ways of the world, you will not only be rooted in hope, but your life will become a living miracle to others and provide a testimony of what it means to be the faithful servant.

As we await our Master's return, we need to prepare daily: pray, seek and find our King, Brother and Friend knocking at our door. As we prepare for His return, we shall choose to live with hope--for our Father is pleased to give us the kingdom (Luke 12:32).

Reflecting on the reading:

1. *What state is your home in? Your family? Your heart? Your faith?*

2. *How can you prepare daily for the Master's return?*

3. *How can you choose to live in hopeful anticipation of Christ's return?*

Weekly readings: Wisdom 18:6-9; Psalm 33:1, 12, 18-22; Hebrews 11:1-2, 8-19; Luke 12:32-48

Out of the Pit

-ASHLEE LUNDVALL

And so they took Jeremiah and threw him into the [pit] of Prince Malchiah, in the court of the guard, letting him down by rope. There was no water in the [pit], only mud, and Jeremiah sank down into the mud.

JEREMIAH 38:6

Growing up in rural Indiana, I had an idyllic childhood. I enjoyed a loving family, great friends, and the ability to maintain a 4.0 GPA while being a four-sport athlete. I rarely felt fear, stress or pain. I did not know loss or heartbreak; life was good. All of that changed during the summer of 1999.

While attending a youth camp at a ranch in northwestern Wyoming, I fell from a hay rack and landed on the wooden handle of the pitchfork I had been using to feed livestock just moments before. The trauma blew out my back at the T-12 vertebrae and permanently damaged my spinal cord. I was sixteen years old, I had my entire life ahead of me, and I would never walk again.

To say it was the darkest time of my young life is a bit of an understatement. I had always been the "good girl." I never caused my parents a moment of grief, I maintained excellent grades in school and if there was a poster child for what a Christian teenager should look like from the outside, I would have been it. Which is why, when my accident happened, I felt so betrayed by God. I had always done everything that I thought He required of me; why was He suddenly reneging on our arrangement and giving me more than I could handle?

Just like Jeremiah, I was in the pit, sunk into the mud. I battled feelings of hopelessness, betrayal and apathy. I had so many ideas and dreams for my future and living my life from a wheelchair was definitely not on my list of goals. God had promised me that He had wonderful plans for my life; surely being disabled wasn't one of them? The pit was cold and lonely.

I will never forget the day when my vision for my life changed. After a particularly difficult morning in the rehabilitation hospital, I finally realized that my accident hadn't just affected my life; it had permanently altered my family's life as well. In that shared pain, I came to understand that I wasn't alone, and that my family was right there with me in the pit, ready and willing to help me climb out.

But I needed more than just the love and support of my family. I had to remember that God had also promised to never leave or forsake me, even in the pit. If I was honest with myself, I knew that He had never strayed, never changed. In my grief and pain, I was the one who was wallowing in the muddy pit. I was too absorbed in my own hurt and heartache to wipe the sludge from my eyes and look to the One who wanted to help me rise. I had a choice to make, and this realization made all the difference in the world.

My climb out of the pit wasn't easy or even consistent. Just when I thought I was gaining ground, my feet would slip in the grime of doubt and fear and I would lose momentum. Any attempt to inch upwards in my own strength was exhausting and futile. The only progress I made was when I stopped fighting and reached out to my Father. He cleared my path and taught me so many lessons along the way, lessons that aided me in preventing a backwards descent.

Looking back nearly twenty years later, I know that the pit still looms just outside my door. I have seen many friends and family members slip towards its dark maw. I have been blessed through pulling others away from its grasp, and have been broken to realize that some have made their home in its depths.

For me, my time in the pit ultimately strengthened me and brought me closer to a loving Savior. I can now fully appreciate the beautiful words of Psalm 40:2: "He drew me up from the pit of destruction, out of the miry bog, and set my feet upon a rock, making my steps secure." And though I may never walk again, I am blessed to live a life with my feet standing fully on the Rock of my salvation.

Reflecting on the reading:

1. *When you think back on your childhood, what idyllic memories do you have?*

2. *What experiences in your life have thrown you into the "pit" of darkness?*

3. *How can you live your life fully standing on the Rock of your salvation?*

Weekly readings: Jeremiah 38:4-6, 8-10; Psalm 80:2-4, 18; Hebrews 12:1-4; Luke 12:49-53

Fixing my Gaze on Jesus
-MICHELE FAEHNLE

Praise the Lord, all you nations! Extol him, all you peoples!
His mercy for us is strong; the faithfulness of the Lord is forever. Hallelujah!

PSALM 117:1-2

As I reflected on these Scriptures for today's reflection, I pondered over the many good times of my life. I have experienced many seasons of great joy, blessings and new beginnings filled with faith, hope and love. When times are good, it is easy for me to read Scriptures of praise and rejoice with an overflowing heart. It is effortless to pray and praise when life is good. Yet, life also brings times of sadness and difficulty. During these times, the praise that comes from my mouth seems hollow and my Hallelujah is weak.

Yet, it is through these times that I have come to understand true hope.

The Catechism of the Catholic Church shares with us that hope is the theological virtue by which we desire the kingdom of heaven and eternal life as our happiness, placing our trust in Christ's promises and relying not on our own strength, but on the help and grace of the Holy Spirit (CCC 1817). It is a gift, given to us at baptism and the "anchor of the soul" (Hebrews 6:19).

St. Catherine of Siena writes, "Hope comes from love" (Letter T352) and it is hope that has given me an eternal perspective on life, helping me hold my head up and look to the heavens when the weight of the world is pressing me down.

Yet even with this awesome gift of hope, sometimes suffering and death may be more than we think we can bear.

This summer, grief came into my life like a Mack truck. The sudden loss of my uncle to a terrible disease, a tragic death of a colleague, and another young mother lost to cancer, all within a week. I suddenly found myself experiencing severe anxiety. Normal activities became challenging for me; driving in the car, pushing the cart in the grocery store, doing the laundry and the dishes, even resting my head on the pillow would trigger a paralyzing and gut wrenching fear to overcome me. I would breathe deeply and pray a Hail Mary or "Jesus,

I trust in You" to get me through the moment. And though I received a short respite, the anxiety always returned. I did not know how to shake this anxiety and I feared I would fall into despair.

St. John Vianney once wrote, "When tempted to despair, I have only one resource: to throw myself at the foot of the tabernacle like a little dog at the foot of his master" (Chervin, Quotable Saints, CMJ Marian Publishers, p 63). Each day, I would go to mass and pray before the Blessed Sacrament, Christ Himself, present in our midst. I would beg Jesus to fill me with hope and peace, and to take away the terrible anxiety that was gripping me.

As I looked up at the large crucifix hanging from the ceiling, I felt His eyes looking down upon me and telling me "Do not to be afraid, Michele; come to me." I knew the source of peace was resting in His heart and no matter what trial and tribulation came before me, He was the reason for my hope. As the days went on and I spent time with Jesus, the anxiety slowly began to lift. I came to understand that if my gaze was fixed upon Jesus I had nothing to fear.

A few days later, I received a sympathy card in my mailbox. The words written on the front were those from St. John Paul II: "Never, ever, give up on HOPE, never doubt, never tire, and never become discouraged. Be not afraid." What a gift! I knew it was a special message from Jesus, and that my friend was prompted by the Holy Spirit to send me this note. Along with it came great consolation and peace. Even in a time of sadness, it was time for me to read these words with great rejoicing: "Praise the LORD, all you nations! Extol him, all you peoples! His mercy for us is strong; the faithfulness of the LORD is forever. Hallelujah!" (Psalm 117:1-2)

Reflecting on the reading:

1. *Are there times in your life when you faced paralyzing anxiety or fear?*

2. *Where did you turn for help? Were you able to overcome the anxiety and fear?*

3. *How can you fix your gaze on Jesus each day, even in the midst of chaos?*

Weekly readings: Isaiah 66:18-21; Psalm 117:1-2; Hebrews 12:5-7, 11-13; Luke 13:22-30

Litanies of Humility and Hope

-FR. NATHAN CROMLY

Humble yourself the more, the greater you are, and you will find mercy in the sight of God.
SIRACH 3:18

Have you ever prayed the Litany of Humility? The prayer beseeches Jesus for the grace to be delivered from the desires of pride and fear of rejection. The prayer asks that we may be delivered from these things so that our relationship with God will be strengthened and become more authentic. Our scriptural passage from Sirach says something similar: "Humble yourself the more, the greater you are, and you will find favor with God."

What is it about humility that is so important for hope and for having a relationship with God?

Humility and hope go hand in hand. In fact, they build off each other! So many of us struggle with being humble, but, in fact, humility is something simple. Humility is about accepting the truth about ourselves. Having a relationship with someone, even a relationship with God, necessitates being able to give ourselves as we really are. When we have the humility to know our true self, we can give that true self and trust that His grace is enough, despite our shortcomings.

Let's be careful, however. Humility doesn't mean letting our weaknesses become our identity; rather, humility means knowing the truth about our strengths and weaknesses and letting God's love for us be our ultimate identity.

Humility helps us to choose hope by letting us relinquish preconceived notions and the desire to be in control. In the poetic narrative "The Portal of the Mystery of Hope," Charles Péguy explores the strange and wonderful role hope plays in the Christian life and finds that the most fitting personification of hope is a little child. He describes how, if Faith and Love are like mature adults steadfastly living their responsibilities to the poor and to God, Hope is like a child who runs ahead of them on the path, amazing even God with her ability to see and love what has not yet come to pass.

Children remind us that the wisdom we should strive for as adults begins in experience, wonder and a spirit of hope. Rediscovering hope – rediscovering a childlike spirit – allows us to respond joyfully to the constraints of time and work rather than letting those challenges chip away at us. When we realize that we don't need to have everything "figured out," life becomes an awesome experience of mercy, of opening up one's hands and trusting that God's plan for us will be fulfilled. Hope reminds us of what Sirach says, "What is too sublime for you, seek not, into things beyond your strength search not."

If we feel out of touch with hope in our lives, one practical means of rediscovering the virtue is to meditate on the witness of heroic men and women, like St. John Paul II, who gave their lives boldly to God and found happiness in doing so. Consider these words of St. John Paul II, for example:

"Jesus does not say 'no' to the authentic demands of the heart, but only a clear, loud 'yes' to life, to love, to freedom, to peace and to hope. With Him no goal is impossible and even a small act of generosity grows and can lead to change."

Today, let's choose to hope! Our relationships are grounded in the humility of knowing who we are, and hope for heaven is grounded in our humility. We can let God into our vulnerabilities and desires now! Then, contrary to human wisdom's demand for anxious productivity, hope will allow us to rest content in trusting God.

Reflecting on the reading:

1. Meditate on the words of St. John Paul II: "With Him no goal is impossible and even a small act of generosity grows and can lead to change."

2. What does having hope for heaven mean to you?

Weekly readings: Sirach 3:17-18, 20, 28-29; Psalm 68:4-7, 10-11;
Hebrews 12:18-19, 22-24a; Luke 14:1, 7-14

Numbering My Days

-MARIE MONSOUR

Teach us to number our days, that we may gain a heart of wisdom.
PSALM 90:12

Four minutes is all it takes to drive to Parkview Pavilion from my house. In those four minutes, I listened to Catholic radio and heard the meditation for the day. It was late July 2018, and I was going in for what I thought was a routine second mammogram. "They just need a better scan. The first one wasn't sufficient," the doctor had remarked. No biggie. The meditation I had heard on the radio during that four-minute drive focused on the passage in Isaiah 38 where Hezekiah is mortally ill and is told that he is about to die, that he should put his affairs in order; he was not going to recover. Hezekiah pleads with the Lord and the Lord grants his request. He is given fifteen more years to live. The priest's reflection started off, "Put yourself in Hezekiah's place. You are gravely ill and are told you are going to die soon."

As I pulled into a parking spot I was thinking, "Ok God – this message is not for me, RIGHT?"

The mammogram and subsequent ultrasound did indeed show a mass, and I received an almost immediate diagnosis: *"You have breast cancer."* The rest of that appointment was a blur – I left with a handful of papers with names of doctors and nurses and dates for treatment. Immediately afterward, I went out to the car and found the podcast for that radio meditation and listened to it again. *Lord, may your word sink deeply into my heart and mind and may I forever be your servant who hears your word and does it (Luke 11:28).*

Arriving home, I grabbed a load of laundry to fold and went to the back room and shut the door. I sucked in my breath and tears flowed freely. I thought about many of my dear friends who have died from cancer. I especially was thinking of my friend Sarry (her real name is Seraphin, but everyone called her Sarry, except her Irish husband Phil, who affectionately called her his "Indian goddess"). Sarry faced her cancer with great faith, hope and trust in God, despite the fact that she had five young children at home and was in her early forties. I could picture her face, with those shining dark eyes. I sat there in the back room of our home and cried. Fear for my own children and my husband overwhelmed me, but the thought of Sarry gave me courage.

The paperwork I had been given contained the name of the "nurse navigator" that had been assigned to me. The next Tuesday I went in to meet with the surgeon, and met Kari. I said, "Hi, are you Kari?" (I pronounced it like "Carrie.") She replied, "It's Kari; it rhymes with Sarry." My eyes grew wide and my mouth hung open. I was speechless. I looked up to heaven in that moment and truly felt my friend Sarry's presence, holding my hand, telling me it would all be okay, that God is in control.

The day I went for the biopsy, this quote was the meditation of the day in my *Magnificat* magazine: "You are having to bear a large, weighty cross. But what a great happiness for you! Have confidence. For God, who is all goodness, will not test you more than you can bear. The cross is a sure sign that he loves you... If Christians only knew the value of the cross, they would walk a hundred miles to obtain it, because enclosed in the beloved cross is true *wisdom*, and that is what I am looking for night and day more eagerly than ever" (St. Louis de Montfort).

I would later learn that I have Stage IA breast cancer. As of this writing, I've had two surgeries and tests galore with mostly positive news. One thing I know: my life is in His hands. The God of wisdom is leading me home. Whether I have fifteen more years or fifty, the number of my days is known to God alone. And that is enough for me.

Reflecting on the reading:

1. *Have you ever heard a message or a sermon and wondered if God wrote that just for you?*

2. *Have you experienced feeling God's presence in a simple miracle, like the nurse's name sounding like Sarry's?*

3. *Knowing that God numbers your days, how can you find peace in living each one?*

Weekly readings: Wisdom 9:13-18b; Psalm 90:3-6, 12-17; Philemon 9-10, 12-17; Luke 14:25-33

Finding the One

-CHERYL LEDFORD

What man among you having a hundred sheep and losing one of them would not leave the ninety-nine in the desert and go after the lost one until he finds it?

LUKE 15:4

When suffering loss, it is easy to feel like you are wandering in a desert, alone, in pain, and lost. Life-altering loss crashed into my family on May 5, 1979, when my parents were in a fatal car accident. I was fourteen years old when I lost my mom; she was only forty-nine years old when she went home to be with Jesus.

My parents and family members were driving home from a dinner out to celebrate the announcement of expecting their first grandchild. On their drive home, a couple who had chosen to drive under the influence crossed left-of-center and crashed into my parents' car, pinning them against the guard-rail. God, in all His mercy, took my mom home to be with Him instantly. My dad survived, left alone to care for his family of seven kids, with four of us still living at home. Somehow, through the pain, God helped us to keep journeying faithfully forward.

That was thirty-nine years ago, and I miss my mom every day. In the special occasions and in the everyday moments.

No matter our loss, God's love is there. In the midst of our loss, we can sometimes wander, but God is always seeking us, and His desire is to bring us home. In Luke 15:1-7 we read the parable of the lost sheep, where He speaks of leaving the ninety-nine to find one. God desires all His children to be with Him, safe and sound for eternity.

Loss crept back into my life over the years through unexpected, emotional infertility issues, coupled with doctor visits and surgeries, only to discover that my marriage partner chose freedom from his marriage commitment rather than faithfulness. My heart was broken.

My life's dream was to become a mom, the kind I had had: selfless, generous, kind, loving the Lord and her family deeply. But in my world, family could not happen to a now-single woman. Loss of hopes and dreams can derail us or even misguide us; I chose to cling to the Vine. Kneeling at my bedroom window in prayer, I vividly recall my words, asking God to remove my fervent desire to be a mom if that was not His desire for my life. I was choosing to hope in the Lord and trust Him with my future.

Dating seemed an awkward idea for me, but God kindled a love with a long-eligible bachelor, the associate minister at my church. Within six months, we married, both understanding that the blessing of children was unlikely. God, in all His amazing goodness, showed us otherwise. Within a few short months, I was pregnant! And in God's amazing way, my due date was none other than Mother's Day!

Sadly, this pregnancy ended with a miscarriage in the first trimester and we were heartbroken. God was there, amidst the pain, through His Word: "And we know that in ALL things, God works for the good of those who love Him, who have been called according to His purpose" (Romans 8:28). He was the miracle-maker behind the pregnancy to begin with, so we continued to trust Him.

On the morning of our second anniversary, we rejoiced in discovering that I was pregnant again. Our first son was born that November. Then God blessed us abundantly with a second son just nineteen months later. To God be the glory, great things He hath done!

I love being a pastor's wife and the mother of our two amazing boys, now growing into handsome young men. I have to remind myself daily that God's ways are not our ways, and yet His way is always best.

In the midst of loss, it is easy to feel like you are wandering in a desert, alone, in pain, and lost. You can find hope in the knowledge that God is searching for you. He will leave the ninety-nine to come find you. When you can't see a way home, trust that God does, and follow Him.

Reflecting on the reading:

1. *What loss have you experienced in your life?*

2. *Have you felt like you were wandering alone through the loss?*

3. *How can you seek God first, trusting Him and knowing He is searching for you?*

Weekly readings: Exodus 32:7-11, 13-14; Psalm 51:3-4, 12-13, 17, 19; 1 Timothy 1:12-17; Luke 15:1-32

It's All In the Name

-ANONYMOUS

From the rising of the sun to its setting let the name of the Lord be praised.
PSALM 113:3

On New Year's Eve, December 31, 2017, I declared in front of my husband and friends that 2018 would be the "Year of Success" for our family. Was it blind optimism? Perhaps. All I knew was that this fresh, new year ahead of me *had* to be better than the previous one.

Ten days later, our world turned upside down.

My husband, the main financial provider for our family of seven, suffered an intense mental trauma brought upon by an abrupt betrayal from individuals in the religious organization where he worked. The trauma was so significant that it left him completely unable to work. For the next three months, almost all of his waking moments were spent in physical pain and mental anguish while he pursued over one hundred hours of group therapy and ingested hundreds of new pharmaceutical pills.

I never knew mental trauma could be so incapacitating. I felt as if I lost my best friend of twenty-two years. My husband was there in body, but his mind and soul were being boiled alive in my presence as the trauma held a solid grip on his mind. He confined himself to the isolation of our bedroom for weeks on end in a desperate attempt to foster recovery.

I threw myself at the mercy of Our Lord. I begged for the grace to survive this new trial of being the sole functioning parent left in our large and demanding household. Still, there were times when words of prayer failed me. But deep down, I knew I could spiritually reach out for the hem of His garment by praying at the very least His perfect name.

Only God could fuel me precisely the way I needed. On a daily basis, I needed to provide compassionate care to my husband. I had to be fully present for the ongoing needs of the four children still in our care. I had to continue to provide caregiving assistance to my live-in widowed mother. I had to keep up with the daily chores and cooking. And I still had to keep up with my full-time ministry work at home. Still, no matter the drain on my spirit, I chose to praise Our Lord.

Psalm 113 reveals that His name deserves perpetual praise and that it is indeed *blessed.* In this context, blessed means supremely happy. Meaning, His name *is* supreme happiness. There is no higher form of joy. I smirked at the irony, since happiness felt non-existent in my life. Each day, I felt the pain of watching my husband, my love, my other half, my best friend remain shackled like a prisoner to depression, trauma and anxiety. Even though my husband could not initially do so, I chose to praise and offer thanksgiving to Our Lord for the both of us.

Eventually, a ray of hope shined through the darkness and it has continued to grow brighter ever since. We successfully separated ourselves from that organization. We successfully redirected our hope from security in a generous paycheck to security in Our Lord Jesus Christ. We successfully remained loyal to reciting a daily rosary. We successfully began attending daily Mass. We successfully remained active in our work of evangelization. We successfully transitioned to a healthier lifestyle. We successfully adjusted our budget to accommodate the temporary decrease in salary. We successfully created a new career opportunity for my husband that will allow him to more fully use his God-given talents effectively so that he can resume providing for his family. We successfully stayed grounded in our faith in Him.

So 2018 may not have been the "Year of Success" for our family, but it was the year of hope. In the midst of our traumatic, painful experience, we were able to pray, to call on the name of the Lord and to trust in His Word. Through those prayers, we found supreme happiness when we placed our trust in Him.

Reflecting on the reading:

1. *Have you experienced pain caused by a fellow Christian, church members, or a Christian ministry?*

2. *How can you separate what people have done to you from what God has done for you?*

3. *This week, pray for your enemies, pray for someone who has hurt or harmed you.*

Weekly readings: Amos 8:4-7; Psalm 113:1-2, 4-8; 1 Timothy 2:1-8; Luke 16:1-13

A Powerful Contradiction
-ANGEL ALOMA

But Abraham replied, 'They have Moses and the prophets. Let them listen to them.'
LUKE 16:29

The Parable of the Rich Man and Lazarus is both powerful and contradictory. Jesus was an excellent teacher and He proved it in many ways – repetition, relevance to His listeners and His masterful use of storytelling (parables). This idea was not new. In the Hebrew Scriptures there are many references to the importance of taking care of the poor and others warning of the consequences of not doing so. "Whoever oppresses the poor shows contempt for their maker…" (Proverbs 14:31a). Yet Jesus brings the message home with the aid of this dramatic, well-told parable – the rich man is not just comfortable, he sports the purple favored by royalty, not cotton or calico, but "fine linen," and his meals are sumptuous.

Notice he has no name. Why? Because he represents all of us! Jesus does not place Lazarus in a shack or garbage dump, but rather right at the rich man's door, where he cannot be ignored, and yet he is invisible. The description of Lazarus' condition is stomach-churning. He is not only poor and hungry, he is homeless and covered in sores. As if that were not enough, dogs would come and lick those sores! The solution would have been simple, no heroic action required; Lazarus' hunger could have been satisfied by the very scraps that fell from the rich man's table.

Lazarus dies, and "is carried by angels to the bosom of Abraham." The rich man also dies and is sent on a one-way journey to the netherworld, where he is tormented in eternal flames. Now he sees Lazarus with Abraham. Now he recognizes him. Now he needs a favor – one that the Patriarch does not grant. If only the rich man were not blinded by his privileged position, by a complete lack of sympathy, by selective blindness.

If one reads between the lines, it's easy to surmise that the rich man does not receive eternal punishment because he was rich, but rather because he refused to recognize that all possessions are transitory and temporal. Rather than using his wealth to serve Lazarus, as he could have easily done, the rich man became a servant to his wealth - a proud slave to what he mistakenly thought were *his* possessions.

Then comes the matter of the warning. "Then I beg you, father, send him to my father's house, for I have five brothers, so that he may warn them…" (Luke 16:27) and Abraham reminds him that Moses and the prophets had warned them. The rich man responds that they would listen if given a warning from someone who came from the other side to them. Abraham is not swayed by this line of reason and refuses once again.

I started this reflection by calling this parable "powerful and contradictory." The powerful is easy to see. This is indeed a well-told, gut-wrenching story in many ways. The contradiction comes in that Abraham, at the end, makes it somewhat hopeless. If they had ignored Moses and the prophets, what then would make them repent of their heartless ways? What comfort can we all take from a story without a happy ending? What is left other than despair when there is no hope of doing better?

Someone better than Abraham and the prophets. Our Lord Jesus Christ.

There lies the beauty, the hope and the contradiction. This is a love story! Jesus is using a hopeless but forceful story in order to give those who listened to him and all following generations a much stronger warning, a warning that we can all heed, a warning from someone who not only died for the love of us, but who returned from the dead in order that we might believe – that we might live.

Reflecting on the reading:

1. *What comfort can we all take from a story without a happy ending?*

2. *Why is this story of the rich man and Lazarus important for us today?*

3. *How can you pray this week and what action can you take to honor Christ with all you have?*

Weekly readings: Amos 6:1a, 4-7; Psalm 146:7-10; 1 Timothy 6:11-16; Luke 16:19-31

A Reawakening
-TANYA WEITZEL

How long, O Lord, must I cry for help and you do not listen?
Or cry out to you, "Violence!" and you do not intervene?
Why do you let me see iniquity? Why do you simply gaze at evil?
Destruction and violence are before me; there is strife and discord.

HABAKKUK 1:2-3

This scripture reminds me of when I was recovering from an eating disorder. I was numb and fully entrenched in my disorder. God was nowhere. I couldn't eat, sleep or function like a normal human being. I felt worthless, broken and incapable. Not being able to handle even the simplest task, I stayed still, paralyzed. All I had the energy to do was be anxious.

This feeling of anxiety transferred itself into nervous habits, like walking around, the inability to sit still and being thrown off guard at the tiniest noise or interruption. I couldn't think straight, focus or function. I wasn't present for my family, friends or God. He was there all along, but I didn't realize it at the time. Walking around like a zombie, I was lost in a sea of the living.

Prayer was too steep a task for me to manage. My body already didn't have the energy for any emotion, including crying, smiling or laughing. I was literally dying and I didn't know what to do. I knew there had to be a way out and hoped that God would be there on the other side.

At the Arise Retreat of 2017, God sent an answer to my weak prayers. Two sisters from the Children of Mary led a Healing Holy Hour. I had already spoken to both of the sisters for spiritual direction about the demons I was fighting. When I arose from my chair to give it all up to God at the altar, they already knew what it was about. It didn't matter that they knew the specifics, but something about sharing my sinful tendencies with the sisters beforehand made me feel more open to taking the next steps. I cried for the first time in years that night.

After my spiritual experience, I continued to eat more, along with meeting with a therapist, a nutritionist and a spiritual director. I did a lot of crying during those first few months. All the feelings I had been denying surfaced at once, so I couldn't control them and I cried out to God for help. Tears formed from my once-dry eyes for hours a day. The emotion and anxiety overtook me and I couldn't do anything else. I had once spent all my time avoiding my feelings, and during this dark time, all I could do was feel. The feelings rushed over me like waves and I was drowning. I knew God was healing me through my pain and tears. Strength came through my sorrow and I not only survived, but I began to thrive and dream again.

I never fully realized how far my eating disorder had taken me over. For years I realized I had some disordered eating habits that had been learned through example and possibly inherited through genetics. Flooded with emotion, I began to be able to separate myself from my disorder. It was a long hard year, but I am now better off. If God hadn't shown me what I was doing to myself, I might not be here today. I can't and don't want to even imagine what would have happened if God hadn't answered my prayers. I asked for an answer, and the answer was me. I was the broken one and God was there to help heal me.

The extent that my mind was entrenched in such a prison still scares me. When anxiety creeps in, my eating disorder habits tend to resurface a bit. Nowadays, my lapses are nowhere near what they were when I was consumed by my eating disorder. A bad day is just that, a bad day. I no longer feel incapable or like I am barely living. I still have tough times, just like everyone else, but I can handle them with God. He pulled me out of my prison and helped me find life again.

Reflecting on the reading:

1. *Have you ever felt that your mind was entrenched in a disorder, addiction or fear?*

2. *How did you climb out of that trench?*

3. *This week, seek God's divine intervention for those who are still entrenched in sin.*

Weekly readings: Habakkuk 1:2-3; 2:2-4; Psalm 95:1-2, 6-9;
2 Timothy 1:6-8, 13-14; Luke 17:5-10

Mindfully Grateful

-EMILY CAVINS

Jesus said in reply, "Ten were cleansed, were they not? Where are the other nine?"

LUKE 17:17

It would be wonderful if everyone had a thankfulness gene built into their DNA, but instead it is something that has to be learned. Parents repeat, "Say 'please' and 'thank you'" from generation to generation, trying to instill that important trait of thankfulness. We see in the gospel reading that Jesus wonders as well why it is so hard to remember to say thank you.

As Jesus was walking along, a group of lepers called out to him and asked for mercy. Without hesitation, Jesus answered their plea by healing them. At that time, in order to be allowed back into the community, a leper would have to be examined by a priest to get the okay to go back into society. Apparently, nine of the men were Jews, but one was a Samaritan. The Samaritan was the one who returned to thank Jesus. He wouldn't have gone to the Jewish priests for examination so he was not in a hurry to go prove anything. He just accepted the miracle and acknowledged the true healer right away. I would hope that the reason the Jewish lepers did not thank Jesus was because they were so amazed that they ran off to follow Christ's instructions to show themselves to the priests.

What could possibly be a reason why a person would not be thankful for a miraculous healing? Pride, ignorance, bad manners, too busy looking at himself, selfishness, too lazy, distracted. Any one of these things can be present in our lives to send us into the trap of ingratitude. We aren't purposely choosing to be ungrateful, but our lack of awareness of the abundant mercy of God can put us in the ungrateful category. It could be called "unintentional ungratefulness." It doesn't make it less of a bad thing if it's unintentional, but certainly if we aren't aware of it, we're less apt to change it.

There are many trends that encourage us to "stop and smell the roses" or to be more "mindful" or to "breathe." All of these ideas are good, but they stop short of the nobler purpose. Why be mindful or take a deep breath? Just for our own benefit? Those things may help us slow down and lower our blood pressure, but do they take us to the ultimate step of recognizing that Jesus has supplied that air we breathe or that mind we are using to be mindful?

Everything circles back to Jesus, the source of everything we have, everything we are made of and everything we will ever need. His mercy and love pour over us every second and we hardly notice! Next time you stop to be mindful, be mindful of the mercy of God. When we respond with thankfulness, we are better able to see our need and reliance on Christ, which then brings us into a closer relationship with Him. And that reminds us to be thankful, and so the circle continues, drawing us in to the love of God.

The Church's liturgy recognizes that we need to be thankful, and so the Mass is centered on the sacrifice Christ made for us. We can consciously enter in to a community of gratitude and in our small human way, give God thanks for all He does. We can be mindfully grateful. We can be the leper who returned to Jesus to thank Him.

Reflecting on the reading:

1. *How can your prayers include gratitude for the blessings in your life?*
2. *What can you thank God for today? This week? This year?*
3. *How can you share your attitude of gratitude with others around you?*

Weekly readings: 2 Kings 5:14-17; Psalm 98:1-4; 2 Timothy 2:8-13; Luke 17:11-19

Passing Hope Down the Line

-CAROL ZOLLINGER

I raise my eyes toward the mountains. From whence shall come my help?
My help comes from the Lord, the maker of heaven and earth.

PSALM 121:1-2

When our son Levi was three weeks old, the pediatrician called at 7:30 on a weekday morning. "We need to talk," he said. He asked if my husband was home and if he could stay home until the doctor made the drive out to talk to us in person. It took twenty minutes, the worst twenty minutes I've lived through. When he arrived, we all sat in the living room to talk, and I held our three-week-old son as tightly as I could.

Moments later, we knew. It was cystic fibrosis. My mother-in-law, a nurse, despaired when she heard the diagnosis. In the fifties, parents of babies with CF were told they wouldn't live to go to elementary school, and back then, many didn't. I had cousins with CF, and they were now in their twenties. I focused on that.

The doctor explained that CF life expectancy was rising all the time, and we had reason to believe him. Having seen for himself that, while shell-shocked, we were functional, the doctor departed. His schedule that day was likely in tatters, but I will always remember his kindness to the end of my days.

We began telling our family about Levi's CF diagnosis. In our small, close-knit community, as soon as one person heard, the news began flying down telephone wires lickety-split, and soon most everyone knew.

It's strange, but often when you're giving someone difficult news about yourself or your family, you end up acting as comforter. You've had more time with the information; you've gone through the worst-case scenarios, dismissed at least some of them and settled just a bit into the new normal. So you say things like, "We'll figure this out," and "Things are much better than they used to be," and "He's doing great!" When you have a big network, you say that over and over again.

By that evening, I was exhausted. Between telling everyone I knew how much better things were in the CF world today, and working through my own emotional hurricane, I could barely lift my head. When the phone rang at eight that evening, I couldn't bear to talk to one more person. Please, God. Not one more. I was lying flat on my bed, crying, and felt like I had the weight of an elephant sitting on my chest. But my husband brought the phone in to me anyway.

It was my cousin's wife. The mother to those boys with CF who were now in their twenties. She asked how I was, and I could tell she wanted to know. My memories are hazy, but I remember she listened to me sob for 45 minutes. I thought I couldn't talk to one more person, but God sent her to me, right then. God knew I needed one more person, the right person.

My son is now ten years old, and he is doing very well. Life expectancy for CF patients rises all the time, and my hope does not lie in the tables and numbers, but rather in the trust I have in Jesus. My hope is real, true. It is also true that the days are sometimes long, and the treatment routines feel onerous. It is true that I rarely think about the long-term realities of CF, and also true that sometimes I am so overwhelmed by those realities I don't know how to go on.

Yet along the way, we have experienced kindness from nurses, doctors and social workers, and from other parents of CF children. We even experienced kindness from a friend who bought us needed CF medical equipment we could not afford, because it would make our days easier.

This is how we live out our hope, I think. We pay attention. We accept the little nudges to look over there, to notice the elephant on someone else's chest. And we give a little shove of kindness. None of us can move the whole elephant by ourselves. But we can help create some breathing room for someone in need, and we can pass a little hope on down the line.

Reflecting on the reading:

1. *Have there been times in your life when you felt hopeless?*

2. *Who in your life brings you comfort, and shares hope with you? Spouse? Family? Friends?*

3. *What is something you can do this week to reach out to someone else in need and pass hope down the line?*

Weekly readings: Exodus 17:8-13; Psalm 121:1-8; 2 Timothy 3:14-4:2; Luke 18:1-8

A Change that Lasts Forever

-SHARON DEITRICK

He does not forsake the cry of the orphan, nor the widow when she pours out her complaint.

SIRACH 35:17

On the morning of September 11, 2001, the world as we knew it changed forever. We were attacked. The United States of America was assaulted by an enemy we didn't yet know. As our nation watched in horror, the tragedies of that day unfolded, and a crippling fear emerged. Jet liners were used as missiles to attack the Twin Towers, the Pentagon and a 4th plane crashed in Pennsylvania. Parents rushed to schools to pick up their children. Panic took hold of hundreds of thousands of New Yorkers in Manhattan that day as they realized they were stranded on an island with no access to the subway or the bridges to get home. Firefighters, police, port authorities and first responders rushed to the scenes with the greatest recorded loss of life on American soil in one day. It seemed hopeless. Was this war?

I was home ill that day, so I was able to watch the unfolding of this enormous loss of life on television. In shock, and almost by rote, I began to pray. I joined those around the world who turned to Our Blessed Lord Jesus in prayer. As the days passed and the loss reached nearly three thousand, we saw something powerful begin to emerge in the darkness. A light began to glimmer in the form of unity. Families were drawn together, children were praying, churches began gathering, even our divided government came together to pray. "The prayer of the humble pierces the clouds" (Sir 35:17). Our nation's flag was unfurled on many a household, office, school. Churches witnessed record attendance.

And then hope was truly revealed! Nearly 500,000 people were rescued from Manhattan that day by ordinary people who had boats and rallied together to form the largest water evacuation in history. They did it in nine hours! Countless heroic lifesaving acts were performed at the Twin Towers, the Pentagon and aboard Flight 93.

The fourth plane, Flight 93, crashed that day in Somerset, Pennsylvania. This was my meeting place with friends, family and clients. Somerset was the halfway point between Washington DC and Akron, Ohio.

I called to help. All we knew was the plane crashed in a barren area. No one on the ground was injured. A few months later, in Somerset, a friend came to visit and shared that they needed help to prepare for the first anniversary where all the families wanted to be present. I humbly offered to help in any way I could.

As townsfolk gathered, and families of the victims began to join our planning, the truth began to unfold. These casualties were NOT victims, they were heroes! They understood that they were on a suicide mission and CHOSE to act. They gathered information from loved ones at home as they were corralled at the back of the plane. They developed a plan to take back the plane, not allowing it to hit its destination in Washington DC, and to be home for dinner that night. They voted, they prayed, they executed the plan. One of the last recorded messages was Todd Beamer, a Flight 93 passenger, and Lisa Jefferson, a 911 supervisor, praying together The Lord's Prayer. It cost their lives, but no one in the US Capitol Building lost their life that day.

After the first anniversary service, the president signed a bill for the Flight 93 National Memorial. I served on the task force and later on the national campaign. My initiative was "93 cents for Flight 93" and our foundation was named HALO - Hope Always Lives On! Students across our great nation sacrificed in some small way to bring every penny, nickel, dime and quarter together to help build this memorial. They continue to speak of the heroic efforts of forty strangers who sat on a plane, faced tragedy, set all their differences aside and stood as one to show that the prayers of the humble indeed pierced the clouds on 9/11/2001.

These students continue to honor the memory of the heroes of Flight 93 by collecting their coins and sending relief to hurricane and flood victims from Hurricane Katrina to Hurricane Florence! So, yes, on the morning of September 11, 2001, the world as we knew it changed forever… we turned as a nation to God. Let us pray that change lasts forever as well.

Reflecting on the reading:

1. *Where were you on the morning of 9/11?*

2. *How has 9/11 changed your life? Your prayer life?*

3. *How can you humbly turn to God each day this week?*

Weekly readings: Sirach 35:12-14, 16-18; Psalm 34:2-3, 17-19, 23;
2 Timothy 4:6-8, 16-18; Luke 18:9-14

As Near As My Next Breath

-ERIN WIMER

When he reached the place, Jesus looked up and said to him, "Zacchaeus, come down quickly, for today I must stay at your house." And he came down quickly and received him with joy.

LUKE 19:5-6

I've read and heard the story of Zacchaeus climbing the sycamore tree so many times I feel like I could recite it word for word. A wee little man climbs up a tree because he's too short to see over the crowd and he's so desperate to just get a glimpse of the Messiah passing through. Not really much to write home about. But as I started to really think about this well-told story, I thought about what Zacchaeus must have been thinking as he climbed that tree.

Zacchaeus had very obviously heard about Jesus--who He was and what He was capable of. There were so many people crowding the streets that it was impossible for Zacchaeus to see Jesus. I wonder if Zacchaeus thought seeing Jesus might be his only chance for redemption from all the crummy things he did as a tax collector. If the Messiah passed him by without a glance would he lose his only chance of salvation? How anxious he must have felt, wondering if this was it. There he was, just another face in the crowd, aching to see Jesus.

As I think about Zacchaeus and his struggle to see Jesus, it makes me so thankful, so full of hope that even if I can't see Jesus from time to time, He always sees me. I don't have to push through the crowds to talk to Jesus. I don't need to flag Him down. He never overlooks me in the crowd of others fighting for His attention. He doesn't make me take a number to place my prayer requests. I don't get pushed to the end of the line because I have sinned more than others.

No, our Jesus is available all day at all times and He is always waiting for us to talk to Him. Whatever our need and whenever our need, He is there. He's never too busy or too distracted. He's not in the business of taking days off, and that gives me hope.

Just a few weeks ago I was going through a very stressful season of life as a mother of two young children and I thought I was handling it ok, until the panic attack hit. I was out for a walk to relieve some stress and clear my mind when the anxiety overwhelmed me and, all of a sudden, I felt as if I couldn't breathe. As hard as I tried, I couldn't get a full breath of air and that was when I started to panic. I thought for sure that I was going to pass out right there on the sidewalk, all by myself, on this walk of peace.

As I tried to calm myself down, I felt the Holy Spirit nudging me to pray. Since I couldn't breathe very well I simply uttered the words, "Jesus, I need you to be my next breath."

My breathing didn't return to normal right away, but a sense of peace that can only come from Jesus washed over me and I could literally feel a weight lift off of me. My mind and body began to relax. Jesus was right there the whole time—never more than a breath away.

I don't know what I would have done that day had I not responded through prayer, had I not sought Jesus in my most desperate need. Prayer is our most precious and sacred gift because it instantly connects us to Jesus. We don't always get what we need immediately, but we have the assurance that our Maker is always listening and always watching. He knows us, He cares for us, and He wants good things for us.

We have uninterrupted access to Jesus, and we don't need to climb a sycamore tree to see Him.

All we need to do is say His name, and He is there, as near as our next breath.

⚓

Reflecting on the reading:

1. *Can you think of a time in your life when stress and anxiety overcame your every thought? When you had a panic attack?*

2. *How did you handle the stress and anxiety? Who did you confide in?*

3. *How can you take your anxieties to the Lord in prayer daily? How can you seek Jesus first?*

Weekly readings: Wisdom 11:22-12:2; Psalm 145:1-2, 8-11, 13-14;
2 Thessalonians 1:11-2:2; Luke 19:1-10

An Apocalyptic Virtue

-BROTHER RICHARD HENDRICK

One of the brothers, speaking for the others, said: "What do you expect to learn by question-
ing us? We are ready to die rather than transgress the laws of our ancestors."

2 MACCABEES 7:2

Hope is an apocalyptic virtue! I bet you never thought of it that way, so let me explain.

The meaning behind the Greek word from which we get our "apocalypse" is very beautiful. It contains within it the description of the action of pulling back a curtain so that light can get into a dark room. Without light, no matter how good our eyesight is, we cannot see.

When the light of the Holy Spirit shines on the mind of St. John, light shines on the dark obscurity of the Church's struggles. It was a time of persecution and pain, and the light of Jesus illuminated the darkness so the light of eternity could be seen. The darkness was seen as moments of struggle, pain and tragedy, but they were also moments unfolding the mystery of the Kingdom of God which will inevitably end when God is all in all.

In this inner knowing, by this holy light, the Christian community is strengthened to actively choose to hope in the Lord, even in the midst of persecution and pain. Each succeeding generation of the Church has been enabled to do the same as they look to the witness of the past and so come to hope in the future.

Hope, therefore, in the Christian sense, is born of an encounter with the apocalyptic light of the Holy Spirit as it illumines the truth of who we are and what our real, eternal context is. We may encounter this truth daily when we choose to see our lives, messy as they are (and often seemingly just hum-drum and ordinary) in the light of eternity, in the light of the Kingdom. When we do this, we choose to look at our lives and their sometimes dark moments as a beautiful succession of opportunities to bear witness to the One who is the light that the darkness can never overpower.

We see that truth illustrated movingly in our reading from the book of the Maccabees today. On the surface, the witness of the sons and their mother seems futile and their suffering without point. A whole family wiped out for sticking to what could seem, at least from the outside, to be a pointless practice. Yet from the perspective of eternity, there is nothing else that they could have done. You see, they know who God is.

They know His love for their people. They know the covenant of their ancestors with Him and they know, they truly know, that they can always hope in Him. In the apocalyptic light of eternity, they see reality as it actually is and are happy to give up even their own lives to bear witness to their hope in God.

As one of the sons in today's reading states, "Ours is the better choice, to meet death at men's hands yet relying on God's promise." If we can take these wonderful witnesses to faith as our example, then we will also touch the freedom that living in apocalyptic light gives.

There will be, for all of us, times of ordinary difficulty and even times of unimaginable pain and perhaps even challenges to our faithful living that we will have no control over, no way of avoiding.

We are not to fear those moments. Instead we can choose to see them as moments of invitation to deepen our faith, to deepen our love, through the exercise of hope. By choosing hope we live from the perspective of eternity. By choosing hope we recognise the truth of our pain and suffering and our need to overcome it, but we also recognise it as a place of witness, as a place of calling. When we live this way, then we ourselves become little apocalypses in which others can see the divine light pulling back the curtain and letting us see reality as it actually is, held always in the triumphant and pierced hands of Love.

Reflecting on the reading:

1. When have you experienced moments of darkness?
2. Has the hum-drum ordinary part of your life separated you from Jesus?
3. How can you worship Jesus through the ordinary parts of your life and keep an eternal perspective?

Weekly readings: 2 Maccabees 7:1-2, 9-14; Psalm 17:1, 5-6, 8, 15;
2 Thessalonians 2:16-3:5; Luke 20:27-38

Pray, Hope, Don't Worry

-MICHAELA GLAFKE (OF NUN AND NUNNER)

Then he said to them, "Nation will rise against nation, and kingdom against kingdom.
There will be powerful earthquakes, famines, and plagues from place to place; and awesome
sights and mighty signs will come from the sky."
LUKE 21:10-11

"Pray, hope, don't worry." The first time I heard St. Padre Pio of Pietrelcina's famous quote I wanted to love it. Not just because the sound of that idea on the surface seemed really refreshing. I wanted to love it because my husband and I have a devotion to St. Padre Pio and were married on his feast day, September 23rd.

However, the phrase rang a little hollow for me. I had a hard time accepting it. "Is it really that easy?" I pondered and prayed over it, but it didn't seem to help. The more I thought about it, the more I questioned St. Padre Pio's motivation behind those words. "What does he mean? Is he invalidating me and my feelings *any* time I have a*ny* kind of anxiety? Should I always be hopeful and peaceful? Because that's quite impossible right now."

It really is near to impossible for us as fallen humans to not worry, to be always hopeful. How do we react when "nation will rise against nation," and when "there will be powerful earthquakes, famines, and plagues...?" We all have our own personal spiritual earthquakes, famines, plagues, wars. How do we respond when these moments arise in our life? Because they will.

When I first heard that quote, "Pray, hope, don't worry," my husband and I were in the midst of a struggle with infertility. Hope was the worst thing in my mind at the time. Bright plans of starting a family were persistently snuffed out. A monthly cycle of hopes rising and then being crushed was taking its toll. Hope was chronically painful and completely exhausting. I didn't realize it until later, but I had come to resent hope.

After several years of failed attempts at charting, surgeries, diets, medications and supplements to treat the root problem, all my hopes and dreams of being a mom, all my plans and attempts for the health and fertility that comes so easy to others, had been destroyed for me.

I languished privately in my faith for some time, to the point it was becoming increasingly difficult for me to go to parish events or even my own weekly holy hour. During one of those holy hours, after practically dragging myself to the chapel like a rebellious teen on a Sunday morning, I sat down in front of our Lord in the Eucharist and said to Him, "I'm sick and tired of trying to deal with this infertility thing on my own; it's hurting my relationship with You and my husband. I can't carry this cross on my own. I give it to You. I offer it to You." And in that moment, God in His unconditional love and grace, clarified to me what "offering it up" really meant. I couldn't believe I had misunderstood that for so long and I chuckled aloud in my pew.

What I had thought was offering it up to God was, in my mind, another way to say grin and bear it. Then, I finally realized deep down in my soul that "offering it up" actually means to give back *everything* joyfully to the Lord, to relinquish control to Him and to be at peace with His will, knowing that His will is generous and kind and merciful. This realization was a gift I didn't realize I was praying for.

I started to have hope again, and not necessarily hope in having children, because that may never happen. Rather than putting my happiness and hope in having kids, or on my husband or myself, I started to hope in the Lord. I started to value myself based on being His and not on being a mother. And while all things are possible through Him, I know that He will give me more than I have ever hoped for, kids or no kids.

"Pray, hope, don't worry" is not a platitude, it's the formula I use to hope in the Lord and to live in peace in Him.

Reflecting on the reading:

1. *When you have been in a low place, have you felt others speaking to you in faith platitudes?*

2. *How can you truly relinquish control to God?*

3. *How can you live out the desire to "pray, hope, and don't worry" daily?*

Christmas readings: Malachi 3:19-20a; Psalm 98:5-9; 2 Thessalonians 3:7-12; Luke 21:5-19

-JEFF CAVINS

He replied to him, "Amen, I say to you, today you will be with me in Paradise."
LUKE 23:43

When someone becomes a Christian, they are incorporated into the life of the Trinity and can participate in the grace of God on a day-to-day basis. Deeply lodged within the heart of every believer is the hope of the beatific vision, which is to one day enjoy God face-to-face for eternity in heaven. With the beatific vision as our goal, all of life on earth must be a purposefully lived life aimed at perfect conformity to Jesus Christ.

Life in Christ is not primarily a singular relationship with God, but a community experience where we are immersed into a way of life. The Catholic Church is more than a community. It is a family in which we learn, live and celebrate Christ together. The Church in her wisdom has orchestrated this way of life, every day, every week, every month and every year in such a way that the faithful will be more perfectly formed to Christ. In short, the liturgical year of the Church conforms our life to the life of Christ so that we can better realize and experience the saving work of Jesus our Lord.

The life of Jesus is broken down within liturgical seasons and days so that the Christian can live out the life, death, and resurrection of Christ. The Church has given the calendar to the faithful as a means of relating to the saving actions of God. This is not a new invention, but an ancient way of conforming our lives to Christ, the King! It is in the liturgical calendar that the faithful enter into the rhythm of the Church; we enter into the rhythm of the life of the Trinity. The Feast of Christ the King is the last day of the year, which had begun with the Advent season. From beginning to end the calendar focuses not only upon the life of Christ, but also upon His kingdom.

Here's a bit of a walkthrough of the year: First, Advent is a time of twofold preparation for the coming of the King. It is a season to prepare for Christmas, which marks the first coming of Christ, and a season when the heart and mind prepare for the Second Coming of Christ at the end of time.

Next to the yearly celebration of the paschal mystery of Easter, the Church holds most sacred the memorial of Christ's birth when we celebrate the birth of the King. Christmas marks the incarnation, when God became a man and for the first time God walked among us as one of us.

Thirty-three or thirty-four weeks remain in the yearly cycle, Ordinary Time. These days, especially the Sundays, are devoted to the many aspects of the mystery of Christ. In Ordinary Time we learn the teachings of the King and how to work with Him in building His kingdom.

We then turn to Lent as a preparation for the celebration of Easter. Lent runs from Ash Wednesday until the Mass of the Lord's Supper. It is on Ash Wednesday that ashes are distributed, reminding the faithful that it was from dust they came and to dust they will return. During Lent we prepare for the most important actions of the King: His death and resurrection.

The most holy part of the liturgical year is the Easter Triduum of the Passion and Resurrection of Christ. Easter is to the liturgical year what Sunday is to the week - the zenith of celebration, the resurrection of the King. After the Easter season and Pentecost, there is again a period of Ordinary Time that leads up to the triumphant celebration of Christ's eternal kingship.

On this day, the Feast of Christ the King, we collect all the works of Jesus and celebrate His complete victory over death, hell and the grave. Truly, He is the King of Kings and Lord of Lords. In short, every week of the liturgical calendar points to this day, the day that focuses on the fact that no one reigns supreme like our Lord and Savior, Jesus Christ!

And as Christians, we participate in the grace of God on a day-to-day basis, holding onto the hope deeply lodged in our hearts to one day enjoy God face-to-face for eternity in heaven. Praise be to God. Amen.

Reflecting on the reading:

1. *How do you celebrate many of the Christian traditions in the community of faith?*

2. *What Easter or Christmas traditions do you celebrate that focus on Jesus Christ?*

3. *How can you incorporate intentional faith traditions into your family's daily life?*

Weekly readings: 2 Samuel 5:1-3; Psalm 122:1-5; Colossians 1:12-20; Luke 23:35-43

Afterword

After a very unexpected pregnancy at the age of 39, we received news that routine genetic testing on our unborn baby had yielded an abnormal result. We did not know the extent of the genetic anomaly at first. The not knowing actually made it harder. My imagination conjured up the worst possible scenarios. "*So, I will be prepared*." I reasoned. Already challenged by my special needs daughter who will likely require lifelong care, I felt like I was at the edge of a cliff, suspended in time, just waiting for the news that would push me over the edge.

After releasing the devotional *Choose Joy* the previous year, I knew full well that no matter what, I had the power to *choose* the path I would take in this situation. This was an opportunity to *live* the words I had pondered through the process of writing the book. Yet sitting in a small chapel all alone, I was seized by fear. I begged for a miracle.

I knew that our unborn baby's life was beyond my own authority. That God had dominion over my child. Yet in coming to Him as a beggar, I could only hold out my hand as prayers failed me.

If my baby were truly gravely ill, should I ask the Lord to heal our child by bringing her to heaven?

Yet, what kind of mother would wish this? Even with a lifetime of faith and countless scriptures at my fingertips, I was afraid. There in the chapel, I opened one of my favorite books to a "random" page and began to read:

"Once, the mother of a boy who had died at the age of eleven years was admitted to my hospital after a suicide attempt. At the death of her boy she was left alone with her other son who was crippled, suffering from the effects of infantile paralysis. His mother, however, rebelled against her fate. But when he tried to commit suicide together with him, it was the crippled son who prevented her from doing so; he liked living! For him, life remained meaningful." This excerpt is from the book *Man's Search for Meaning* by Austrian psychiatrist Victor Frankl.

In my hour of darkness, it was the hope I needed. My baby was thriving and growing. I thought, "My child wants to live!"

The next day we went to the doctor's office to hear the results of the genetic testing. We were told that our baby likely had Down Syndrome. We also learned our little miracle was a girl. As my husband and my mother looked on, the obstetrician placed the doppler on my 12-week abdomen to see the baby on the ultrasound. There was our precious daughter, measuring *exactly to the day*, but void of a heartbeat.

This is a difficult hope. A life cut short. Dreams unfulfilled. This was my fourth miscarriage and like the others, I was completely helpless to change the situation. But God's pedagogy is perfect.

Already having one special needs child has taught me so much. We are all carrying wounds and loss. Some are more visible than others. My autistic daughter has a disability that is obvious. Some people do not want to get too close; they are afraid to touch the wound and so they stay at arm's length. But Jesus invites us. There is great power there.

This is the message of salvation and the paradox of the cross. In conceptualizing this book, it is the final message I pray resonates. Jesus was crucified on Good Friday; He was paralyzed unable to even receive hydration. The "King of the Jews" hung in a crucified clump, disabled and defeated. But it was precisely THEN that He was never more potent. Through His suffering He completed the mission He was sent to accomplish-to save us all!

"He whose power is at work in you is powerful enough and more than powerful enough to achieve HIS designs beyond all your hopes and dreams." *(-Ephesians 3:20)*

We named our unborn baby Joy Hosanna. Quite literally, we chose Joy. Her brief life gifted our family with the reminder that whether we live three months, thirty-three years or to one hundred and three, every life has meaning and purpose and every hardship can be used for the glory of God. But while I had spent the previous year in the study of joy and orienting my heart to choose eternal joy, it was still very difficult when I was cast down and struggling. I share this as an admission that this book may not be a perfect panacea. We pray it is a start though, however small, to inspire endurance as we meet the challenge of each hour.

It is a uniquely human (and blessed) trait to be able to turn tragedy into triumph. As believers, we follow in the footsteps of our Redeemer in this way.

To be clear, hope is different from optimism. Jerry Groopman, M.D., in his book, *The Anatomy of Hope says:* "Hope does not arise from being told to 'think positively,' or from hearing an overly rosy forecast. Hope, unlike optimism, is rooted in unalloyed reality. Hope is the elevating feeling we experience when we see a path to a better future. Hope acknowledges the significant obstacles and deep pitfalls along the path. True hope has no room for delusion. Clear-eyed, hope gives the courage to confront our circumstances and the capacity to surmount them. For all my patients, hope, true hope, has proved as important as any medication I might prescribe or any procedure I might perform." *(pg. 14)*

Stories of human achievement in spite of great odds remind us that all we need to keep going is *the next breath*. There is no soul beyond redemption. The devil's mission is to discourage us. To whisper the lie that we are beyond hope. We must not fall into this trap. There is *no one* so lost that he/she cannot be filled with God's peace and power (Psalm 139: 1-12).

The story of Noah's endurance shows us. Piece by piece he persevered to build the life-saving vessel that he hoped would withstand the flood. Even though he may have looked deranged to bystanders, he continued to show up. His obedience and effort was rewarded. Day by day, we too have the power to choose hope, press on and bear witness to God's redemptive work in our lives. To bring meaning through our crosses. We know that our ultimate hope does not lie in this world. It is in Christ, the author and perfecter of our faith.

My friend, Pastor Linda Isaiah, often speaks about the phenomenon of what she calls "Different, better and more." It is the idea (illusion rather), that we would just be happy if circumstances around us would change. But this is in error if we truly believe that God is capable of utilizing everything for the good. Father Jacques Philippe illuminates this concept in his book *Searching for and Maintaining Peace*: "God may allow me occasionally to lack money, health, abilities and virtues, but he will never leave me in want of Himself, His assistance and His mercy." *(pg. 43)*

May we cling to the anchor of our soul with the certitude that the Reason for our Hope is preparing "what eye has not seen, and ear has not heard" for us, as His beloved children and heirs of eternal hope.

Choose Hope Contributing Authors

Angel A. Aloma – Angel serves as executive director of Food For The Poor (www.foodforthepoor.org). Angel was a Catholic school teacher before joining the charity in 2001. He was educated primarily by Jesuits and priests of St. Basil. For five summers, Angel traveled with his students to do missionary work in the Dominican Republic. He lives in South Florida with his wonderful wife of 47 years. They have three sons, two nieces who are daughters and nine beautiful grandchildren.

Corina Barranco – Corina was born in a small town in Mexico. Her parents migrated to the United States when she was five. She attended Sacred Heart Chapel where she currently serves as an altar server. Corina was featured in a *Time Magazine* article, sharing about her experience and DACA. She currently works at McDonalds and attends Lorain Community College where she is working toward a Bachelor's Degree in social work.

Caitie Rose Beardmore (Sister Mary Rose of Nun and Nunner) – Caitie is the campus minister and senior theology teacher at Central Catholic Jr/Sr High School in Lafayette, Indiana and one-half of the Catholic comedy duo "Nun & Nunner." Caitie has a BA in pastoral theology from Marian University and, as the oldest of eight children, has been doing youth ministry since she was in diapers. Caitie's passion is sharing the faith with people through humor, storytelling and song!

Hannah Berg – Hannah is a graduate student studying occupational therapy at Walsh University. She has traveled as a missionary to Haiti two times through Haitian Christian Outreach and throughout Southeast Asia, including Cambodia and Myanmar through her work with Southeast Asia Prayer Center out of Pittsburgh, PA. Her career goal is to work in pediatric occupational therapy with children who face physical and emotional challenges.

⚓

Dr. Trish Berg – Trish is a published author of two books, co-author of four books, a former newspaper columnist and speaker for MOPS and Hearts at Home. She serves as an assistant professor of business at Walsh University in Ohio where she focuses on growing her faith, mentoring her students, researching leadership and resiliency, and shining the light of Christ to those around her. Trish and her husband, Mike, have four children ages 23 to 16.

Theresa Blackstone – Theresa is a blogger at ordinarylovely.blogspot.com, and shares bits of this blessed life on Instagram @ordinarylovely. She is a wife, mother, and homeschool mom of five. She is mother to baby Monica Jane who passed away shortly after birth in February of 2018.

Emily Cavins – Emily is the author of *My Heart is a Violin; Lily of the Mohawks: The Story of St. Kateri; A Pilgrim's Guide to the Church of the Holy Sepulchre*; and co-author of *The Great Adventure Storybook: A Walk through the Catholic Bible*. She received her degree in Classical and Near-Eastern Archaeology from the University of Minnesota and leads pilgrimages with her husband Jeff to the Holy Land and other Bible related places. Info at www.jeffcavins.com.

Jeff Cavins – Jeff is an evangelist, author, and biblical scholar. He is the creator of *The Great Adventure Bible Study* program and was the founding host of the television show "Life on the Rock" on EWTN. He is an author of dozens of books and speaks about scripture around the world. He is the host of the popular podcast *The Jeff Cavins Show*.

Miguel Chavez – Miguel serves as associate vice president for mission implementation at Walsh University where he also serves as an adjunct professor in theology and is the author and creator of the *From Water into Wine* young adult ministry program. Miguel is a speaker and facilitator for retreats and formation programs. He is married to Walsh DPT alumnus Dr. Kristen Chavez and they have three beautiful children, Avery, Tessa, and Isaiah. For more information see: https://www.walsh.edu/miguel-chavez.

Ruth Clifford – Ruth is wife to David and stay-at-home mom of three beautiful boys. She is a writer and businesswoman. Ruth is passionate about God, her family, and ice cream.

Fr. Nathan Cromly, CSJ – Nationally renowned Catholic leader and Brother with the Community of Saint John, Father Cromly has worked in youth ministry, teaching, retreat preaching, book publishing, and has served as Prior of his community's house in Laredo, Texas. Father Cromly is also the founder and president of Eagle Eye Ministries and Saint John Institute. He has spoken at retreats and taught in diverse settings including Iceland, England, Hawaii and Ireland.

Sharon Deitrick – Sharon is the founder of The HALO Foundation – Hope Always Lives On – that teaches students servant leadership, inspired by the heroes of Flight 93. She loves the Poor Clares of Perpetual Adoration and assists with their foundations in Cleveland, OH, Troyes, France, and now Canton, OH. https://thehalofoundation.org/

Amy Dodez – Amy is a mother of two and wife to Mark. Mark and Amy's daughter, Karrie, went to be with the Lord when she was nine years old. Their son, Steven, is a freshman in college at Slippery Rock University. Mark and Amy are now venturing into the empty nest years and trusting God on this amazing journey of joy and hope.

Rebecca Dussault – Rebecca is a 2006 U.S. Winter Olympian (xc skiing) and 2010 World Champion (winter triathlon), wife, mother, professional athlete, fitness trainer, wellness coach, and motivational speaker.

Michele Faehnle – Michele is co-author of the bestselling, award winning *Divine Mercy for Moms* and *The Friendship Project*. She is the co-director of the Columbus Catholic Women's Conference. Michele blogs at divinemercyformoms.com and is a contributor to catholicmom.com. She is a wife, mother of four, and a school nurse.

Dr. Chad Gerber – Chad and his wife, Jennifer, and their family suffered an unimaginable loss when their 11-year-old daughter, Evie, died suddenly in 2015. Chad grew up in an agricultural family in the Amish-Mennonite region of Ohio, and he earned four degrees in theology and philosophy. He currently serves as an assistant professor of theology at Walsh University in North Canton, Ohio. He is a graduate of the University of Oxford and the author of *The Spirit of Augustine's Early Theology: Contextualizing Augustine's Pneumatology.*

Jennifer Gerber – Wife, and homeschooling mother of five on earth and one in heaven. Jennifer, her husband Chad, and their family suffered an unimaginable loss when their 11-year-old daughter, Evie, died suddenly in 2015. She writes about her grief journey at allsaintsfarm.org.

Eden Gerber – Young writer and daughter of Dr. Chad and Jennifer Geber, Eden shares about choosing to hope after losing her best friend and sister, Evie, in 2015.

Michaela Glafke (Sister Maria Stella of Nun and Nunner) – Michaela and her husband, Mark, (a Catholic clinical psychologist) both graduated from Purdue University. Michaela is the administrative assistant on the campus ministry team at Lafayette Central Catholic Jr/Sr High School where she works with her BFF and "Sister in crime" in Nun and Nunner. A natural outgrowth of their friendship, Nun and Nunner performs around the country "singing contemporary songs for the Lord."

Lisa Hendey – Lisa is the founder of catholicmom.com and a bestselling author of fiction and non-fiction for adults and children. Her "Chime Travelers" fiction series is read and studied worldwide. A frequent television and radio guest, Lisa's writing has been featured in multiple outlets. Hendey speaks internationally on faith, family, and technology topics. She has traveled worldwide with non-profit organizations to support their humanitarian missions. Visit her at www.lisahendey.com and at @LisaHendey on social media.

Brother Richard Hendrick – Brother Richard is a Capuchin Franciscan priest-friar, living and working in Ireland. He is currently the Guardian of Ards Friary in Donegal which includes a large residential retreat center. (More at www.ardsfriary.ie)

Pastor Linda C. Isaiah – Linda is an international conference speaker. Linda has been featured on TBN, TCT, 95.5 The Fish and numerous other media outlets. She's traveled to Ireland and South Africa preaching and teaching a word of HOPE that is found in Jesus Christ. Linda is a certified grief recovery specialist and has been a member of The House of the Lord in Akron, Ohio for more than 38 years.

Emily Jaminet – Emily is co-author of the bestselling *Divine Mercy for Moms*, *The Friendship Project*, and part of the leadership team of the Columbus Catholic Women's Conference, speaker and radio personality. She is a regular blogger at divinemercyformoms.com and contributor to catholicmom.com. Jaminet holds a B.A. from The Franciscan University of Steubenville in mental health and human services and a minor in human life studies.

Cheri Keaggy – Recognized as a mainstay in Christian music for nearly twenty-five years, Cheri has released nine albums garnering nine number one songs, three Dove Award nominations and a Dove Award win. It is her mission to share Christ, ministering His message of hope and healing through song, speech, and the written word. Cheri has two adult children, one grandson, and lives with her husband and two dogs in Franklin, TN. Visit for Music/Tour/Blog/Speaking: www.cherikeaggy.com.

Dr. Philip Kim – Phil is an author, speaker, and professor. As the son of first-generation Korean immigrants, Phil learned the value of hard work at an early age. He has worked at every one of his parents' businesses including diners and lunch trucks and various convenience stores. He is the author of *Chase One Rabbit* and *Zebras & Ostriches*. Phil continues to teach full-time as a business professor at Walsh University. His website address is: http://write15minutes.com.

Gail Knarr – Gail lives in Pittsburgh, Pennsylvania with her husband, Brian, where she has worked as a preschool teacher and as a nanny and is currently an office administrative assistant for her church's children's ministry. Her faith in Christ has led her down many unique paths, including serving as a Christian camp counselor, church drama director, and mentor mom for her local MOPS group. She also loves crafting and participating in community theater.

Elena LaVictoire – Elena has been married to her high school sweetheart for over 30 years. They have six children (from 29 to 13) who were all homeschooled. For the past nine years, Elena has been recording and performing with the Peace Together Choir (hopefulmusic.com). When she's not homeschooling, practicing her flute or playing with her five-year-old granddaughter, she blogs regularly about her issues and events that affect her family at mydomesticchurch.com.

Cheryl Ledford – Cheryl is a CPA, faithful wife and mother of two teenage sons, Carson and Dylan. Married for 21 years, Tom is associate minister at Orrville Christian Church, and they reside in Apple Creek, OH. Cheryl volunteers her time with school organizations and serves in various ministries at OCC. Through loss, Cheryl learned the immense value of family and that holding onto Jesus will see you through the toughest of times.

Dr. Donald A. Lichi – Donald is a licensed psychologist and serves as vice president of EMERGE Counseling Services in Akron, OH. He has been a speaker at numerous conferences and workshops on pastoral health, Christian education, parenting, marriage, and family issues. He is the co-author of the book, *Broken Windows of the Soul* (Moody Press). Best of all, he is married to Marcie and they have three adult children and seven grandchildren.

Marcia Lichi – Marcia lives in Ohio with her husband of 47 years, Dr. Don Lichi. They are blessed with three children and seven grandchildren. Marcia is a Spanish teacher at Cuyahoga Valley Christian Academy. She enjoys sharing her love of Spanish language and culture with her students. Marcia came to faith in Christ at the age of 15 and has found Him to be a faithful and true Savior.

⚓

Kelly Lilak – Kelly is a woman in love with our Lord, His Church, our faith, His Mother and His people. After graduating from BGSU with an early education degree, Kelly traveled to Haiti where she worked in an orphanage with Mother Teresa's sisters. Her career includes working with local youth groups and women's conferences. She is currently giving a year of service at an NPO in the Cleveland area, living in community with other women and growing closer to God. You can find Kelly on Facebook.

Pam Lile – Pam is a wife and homeschooling mother of 8. Married for 17 years, she and her husband juggle the demands of family with their evolving business ventures. Pam has been instrumental in establishing a club for girls at her parish. In June of 2018 her son suddenly suffered a stroke. Pam began a blog of sorts on Facebook to inform others of Sam's progress. Her writing is full of hope and is an inspiration to many.

Ashlee Lundvall – Ashlee Lundvall was crowned Ms. Wheelchair USA in 2013. She is author of *A Redefined Life*, is a national pro staffer for Mossy Oak, and a member of the NRA's Disabled Shooting Sports and Outreach committees. She received the 2017 SCI Foundation Pathfinder Award. Ashlee has her master's degree in biblical counseling and was appointed to the President's Council on Sports, Fitness & Nutrition. Ashlee lives in Wyoming with her husband and daughter and can be reached at www.ashleelundvall.com.

Melody Lyons – Melody is a happy wife and homeschooling mother of eight who also moonlights as an author, speaker, natural health care advocate, and entrepreneur. As a chronic illness survivor and thriver, she writes about healing of the mind, body, and soul in the context of a free, faithful, joyful life in Christ. She can be found writing and dreaming at her website, The Essential Mother (theessentialmother.com).

Yolanda Maldonado – Yoli is married to her sweetheart Marcos. They met at church as teenagers, went their separate ways, but found their way back to each other and now have two children, Jesse and Nila. Another thing they share in common is that both their fathers were ordained as deacons by the Diocese of Cleveland, Ohio. Yoli is a stay-at-home mom with a beautiful faith-filled journey that she is happy to share with her family.

Autumn Mankins – Autumn is a faithful mother of two children (Anna Beth, 3 and Luke, 1) and wife to Steve. She does stage design at Orville Christian Church and co-hosts a Bible study for stay-at-home moms. She and her husband are small group leaders for young married couples. Autumn enjoys hosting craft workshops at a local community center for busy moms like herself.

Kate Medina – Kate is a graduate of Ashland University, where she met Jesus and her "hot tamale" husband, Jose. They live on a five-acre slice of country in Ohio with their four witty children and two unruly doodle dogs. Kate adores bare-faced honesty, gathering people, and chips with guac. Sometimes she writes, spilling gutsy truth and epic grace in equal measure.

Dr. Angela Miller – Angela is a Catholic wife, homeschooling mom, clinical psychologist, and science enthusiast. In her elusive free time, she loves to read and collect fancy pieces of paper from institutions of higher learning. She lives in Canton, Ohio, with her exceedingly patient and supportive husband and their four young children.

Marie Monsour – Marie is a wife and mother to 10 children. Marie was diagnosed with early stage breast cancer in July 2018. With medical care and prayer, she has great hope for the future. She homeschools her youngest four children and volunteers her time in various ministries including St. Gabriel Media and Little Way Homeschool Co-op. With God's grace, she still laughs at the days to come. Marie and Dave and their family reside in Northeast Ohio.

Pastor John Mulpas – John was born and raised in Ohio and is a graduate of Cincinnati Christian University (CCU). During his time at CCU John decided to pursue full-time Christian ministry. Currently he serves as lead pastor of Orrville Christian Church in Orrville, Ohio. John's passion is to "Preach the Word...with great patience and careful instruction." (2 Timothy 4:2). John is married to Beth, and together they have three children.

Christina Nieto – Christina is a former stay-at-home mom who recently returned to work after eight wonderful years caring for her children. During her life she's overcome many circumstances by choosing hope. She is married to her wonderful husband and loves being mom to Elena and Elliot.

Mark Piccolino – Mark has been a Christian practically all of his life. He is a business owner of Crescent Gardens Floral Shoppe, east of Pittsburgh. He is married to Barb, and they have three children and four adorable grandchildren. He loves spending time with his family, enjoys singing and some cooking. He has been a prayer partner at his church for the past 13 years.

Vicki Przybylski – Vicki is a police officer who is married to her hero Nik, also a police officer. They have three beautiful children. Vicki enjoys volunteering for youth group, PTU and Girl Scouts. She is a proud member of the St. Gabriel Media team and enjoys reading in her free time.

Betty Schnitzler – Betty is a Catholic wife, married to Greg for 37 years, mother of three adopted children, one son-in-law and grandmother to Eleanor. She is retired and blessed to be able to help take care of Eleanor after school. Betty is passionate about pro-life issues and enjoys spending time with her sisters in Christ from her parish and other Christian groups.

Joan Mary Spieth – Joan hails from Sandusky, Ohio. Born the last in a family of ten, her singular dream and hope from the age of seven was to become a Sister at Notre Dame. For her high school career and canonical year, that is where she was. Withdrawing from the convent set her on a new path that led to marriage, motherhood, grand-motherhood, and widowhood. She has written now and then, mostly poetry. *Poems by Joan Mary* is her one published work.

⚓

Emily Tappe – Emily is a busy mom of two preschoolers (Brody and Blake) and wife to Matt. She is a stay-at-home mom who has served as a special education paraprofessional for elementary school age children. She graduated from Malone University in Ohio, and currently lives in Pittsburgh, Pennsylvania, where she stays actively involved in her church and with family and friends.

Brooke Taylor – Brooke is a speaker, radio personality, host of Good Things Radio podcast, writer, and founder of Saint Gabriel Media, LLC. Along with her amazing team, Brooke hosts the Arise retreat, aimed at building a sisterhood of believers for Christ. For nearly a decade, Brooke Taylor was co-host of the "Family Friendly Morning Show" on 95.5 The Fish in Cleveland, Ohio. Brooke's greatest "gig" is wife and mother to five children.

Ben Walther – A singer, speaker and published songwriter, Ben has traveled extensively over the last 15 years. He has frequently presented and led worship at diocesan and regional events, including Life Teen and Steubenville conferences and camps. A graduate of Franciscan University of Steubenville, Ben is honored to now serve the Walsh University community as the director of campus ministry. He and his wife, Maria, and children live in North Canton, Ohio.

Maria Walther – Maria has been married to her college sweetheart for 17 years and together they have six beautiful children on earth and two in heaven. Maria has a heart for those who have suffered the loss of a child through miscarriage, and she uses this passion for the beauty and sanctity of life in her online prayer ministry.

Tanya Weitzel – Tanya lives with her husband and son in Connecticut. She is a wife, mom, homemaker, homeschool teacher, library assistant, and writer. She contributed to *The Catholic Mom's Prayer Companion: A Book of Daily Reflections* and *Choose Joy: A 52-Week Devotional Journey*. She enjoys walking, reading, and a good cup of coffee. She can be found at startingfromscratcheveryday.com.

Dr. Anne Valeri White – Anne is a Catholic family physician, wife, and mom of four daughters. She is on the Saint Gabriel Media team, and also contributed to the *Choose Joy* devotional. Fueled by coffee and Jesus, she has been practicing and teaching Family Medicine for ten years. Anne's passions include caring for new moms in addiction recovery (and their babies), obstetrics, physician burnout, osteopathic manipulation, narrative medicine, and works of mercy.

Erin Wimer – Erin is a busy mom of two young kids, Grace and Landon, and wife to Tony. Alongside her husband, Erin works part-time at Southeast Asia Prayer Center as the Raising Kids Coordinator. She graduated from Malone University in Ohio and currently resides in Pittsburgh, Pennsylvania. She is actively involved in her church and works part-time on the children's ministry team. In her free time she loves to read and spend time with her family and friends.

Carol Zollinger – Carol lives and writes on a small farm in northeast Ohio, where she and her husband raise beef cows and young boys. You can find more of Carol's work at www.thecircusishere.com.